OUR
VIOLENT
PAST

An American Chronicle

OUR VIOLENT PAST

An American Chronicle

IRVING J. SLOAN

Preface by Ramsey Clark,
Former Attorney General of the United States

 RANDOM HOUSE · NEW YORK

Acknowledgment is gratefully extended to the following for permission to
reprint from their works:

E. P. Dutton & Co.: From *Narrative of Riots at Alton*, by Edward
Beecher, introduction by Robert Merideth.

Life: "Race War in Detroit" as it appeared in the July 5, 1943, issue.
Copyright 1943 by Time, Inc.; "Battlefield: Where the Law Won" as it
appeared in the October 5, 1962, issue.

Oxford University Press: From *The Boston Tea Party*, by Benjamin
W. Labaree.

Stanford University Press: From *Origins of the American Revolution*, by
John C. Miller.

Southwestern Historical Quarterly: From "Law & Lawlessness on the
Texas Frontier," by William C. Holden, Vol. XLIV (1940).

California Folklore Society: From *Western Folklore*, Vol. VI, No. 2, pp.
115-118. Copyright 1947 by the California Folklore Society.

California Folklore Society: From *Western Folklore*, Vol. XII, No. 4,
pp. 229-241. Copyright 1953 by the California Folklore Society; reprinted by permission of the Society and the author, Austin E. Fife.

University of North Carolina Press: From *Prologue to Revolution*, by
Edmund S. Morgan, published for the Institute of Early American
History and Culture; from "Pattern of Violence," by H. C. Brearley
in *Culture in the South*, edited by W. T. Couch.

Routledge & Kegan Paul Ltd.: From *The American Indian Frontier*,
by William C. Macleod.

Fortune: From "The Industrial War" as it appeared in the November,
1937, issue.

Russell & Russell: From *The Story of the Mormons from the Date of
Their Origin to the Year 1901* (1902), by William Alexander Linn.

Literary Digest: October 18, 1919, pp. 9–11. Courtesy of Time, Inc.

LIBRARY OF CONGRESS CATALOG CARD NUMBER: 70-85617

MANUFACTURED IN THE UNITED STATES OF AMERICA BY
HADDON CRAFTSMEN, INC., SCRANTON, PA.

9 8 7 6 5 4 3 2

FOR JERRY AND PATTY BOCK,
IN FRIENDSHIP.

TO THE LATE MARTIN LUTHER
KING, JR., WHOSE WORK AND WORDS
REMAIN A SOURCE OF HOPE THAT
OUR VIOLENT PAST IS PAST AND HIS
MESSAGE IS FUTURE.

ACKNOWLEDGMENTS

To Joe Mintzer, I owe the appearance of this work. His assistance from the time it was an idea to the time of publication was invaluable.

To Alan Westin and Ray Smith of Columbia University's Center for Research and Education in American Liberties, I am thankful for the time and facilities they made available to me to work on the book while I was still associated with the Center's Summer Institute for Advanced Study for Teachers during the summer of 1968.

To Bob Bernstein, a very special kind of gratitude for the warm enthusiasm of his support as my publisher.

Finally an expression of appreciation to my wife and son, Esther and Philip, for enduring patiently and even graciously the time I spent away from home responsibilities, always so inevitable in the writing of a book.

I.J.S.

PREFACE

This is not a happy chronicle. America has had a violent past as it has a violent present. Still it is well to study these tragic events, not out of a fascination with their wild emotion or a curiosity about their cruelty, but that we may know ourselves. For violence is the antithesis of human dignity. As no other act of man, it demeans both the worth of the individual and the civilizing influence of compassion. Violence cheapens life and scorns reason. A people who are concerned about their character or care for their future must know their capacity for violence. Only when we know ourselves can we come to grips with violence. Until then frenzied reaction, and not reason, will guide our effort. And finally we must act to still the fury in our hearts.

The violent events described in this book are edited from a long and diffused history involving all of our people, dealing only with a fraction of the group violence we have suffered. It does not intend to touch on the pervasive personal violence—murder, assault, mugging, rape, and robbery—that destroys life, livelihood, family, faith, and hope. Nor can it relate the institutional and social violence that causes despair, rage, and psychosis by forcing poverty, ignorance, sickness, discrimination, idleness, crime, and injustice on powerless millions. War and other so-called legitimate uses of violence are foreign to its scope. But the reader must keep all these in mind. For while we are conditioned to know and accept violence in some forms, we must learn to expect it in others.

This history catalogs many of the major occasions on which Americans with a common purpose have used violence to achieve or prevent change. These are case studies of group violence as a social-problem solver: the wresting of lands from the Indians, the legal, economic subjugation and social emancipation of the Negro, the enforcement of order in the frontier vacuum in the absence of a satisfactory police power, the struggle by labor to share in the increased production of industrialization.

However, the violence described in the book actually played a very minor, almost insignificant role as a direct force for change. The real effect of such violence seemed clearly to flow not from the power it applied but from the message it carried. Lethargy and ignorance were so deeply ingrained that awareness of the depths of emotion surrounding a situation was communicated only through the horror of the violence employed. While the immediate public reaction was nearly always abhorrence and repression, the longer-range impact was a loosening of opposition to change, a greater sensitivity to its need, and a growing commitment to its accomplishment.

Whatever the effect of group violence, it was never adequate as a means of coercion or as a cause of change. It added to a general climate of violence and to divisions within the country, and diminished respect for the rule of law and for our institutions. Far more effective and less divisive techniques of social change must be developed if America is to meet the challenge of the future.

Nature conspired to make violence common in America. A frontier, a totally foreign and largely uncivilized aboriginal people, the early development of brutalizing slavery of a different race from a distant continent, pioneers moving beyond the reach of established institutions, the interaction of a wide range of cultural, racial, ethnic, and social backgrounds in a new melting pot, an early and devastating civil war, a tradition of guns, an immense population growth both native and immigrant, vast industrialization and urbanization, high mobility and rootlessness, and sweeping technological development—all these and more contributed to change and to instability beyond that experienced by any other people at any time in history.

In a sense our people were subjected to the trauma of exploring several New Worlds simultaneously—not just the geography of North America but the interrelation of many different peoples from many different countries and continents with wide racial, cultural, and social disparities, and the totally new environment of mass population, high urbanization, and accelerating technological development.

Human nature bore it well. Other people will undergo what America has experienced. We must hope they fare as well. Our group violence in the main has been limited and equivocal. Its motive has been coercion to change or retain, however irrational or vengeful the event. For some people, cruelty or destruction has been an end in itself. America, however, has not seen widespread guerrilla warfare, the slaughter of thousands of innocents, lampshades of human skin, hearts cut out and eaten, or heads carried proudly on poles.

But the question is not really one of comparisons. The question is how we can reduce violence to a minimum. Nor are the needs to reduce violence comparable. Violence has never threatened more than a handful in the past. Today it threatens all. Technology, which has contributed much to the dimension of violence in America, has created a capacity for violence that includes total destruction. In a world sick with violence, emotional and afraid, there is no reason to believe some inner restraint or wisdom which could not deter the club will stop the Bomb. The power of technology and the total interdependence of the individual demand we avoid violence, or we destroy ourselves. For the cave man, violence was essential to survival; for modern man, it promises obliteration.

As we review group violence, it is important to remember the lesson of Martin Luther King, Jr. He lived among a people who suffered most from the fury of America— our black brothers. He knew as only they can the full pity of human violence. He saw violence in the hearts of nearly all around him. He saw injustice visited upon his people as few have borne it before. He sought change with a passion that caused him to dare to walk all his adult years in the Valley of the Shadow of Death. Still he sought change through nonviolent action alone, and no force on earth could taunt him to hurt another or to diminish the dignity of man by violence.

This is what America must do. We must strive for justice with all our might while constantly and consciously controlling our inner impulse to violence. Within the next few years we must make every effort to expunge the capacity for violence from our being.

All the dynamics of our days compel us to strive ardently for change to fulfill the needs of humanity in our mass, urban, technologically advanced society. The two major endeavors of our time must be the implementing of effective social change and the purging of violence from the human condition. And all of our vision tells us we must seek change humanely, in a gentle way with one another, full of compassion and with a reverence for life—mere life—as an end in itself.

Santayana tells us that if we forget our history we are condemned to repeat it. Irving Sloan's reminder of events in our American past which we might too readily choose to forget is an important one, and we can be thankful to have it while we work at the challenge of not repeating it.

RAMSEY CLARK

February, 1970

CONTENTS

LIST OF
ILLUSTRATIONS

OUR
VIOLENT
PAST

An American Chronicle

"Hurt nothing unless you're forced to," yet Cooper's Deerslayer got his deepest thrill of gratification perhaps, when he puts a bullet through the heart of a beautiful buck, as it stoops to drink at the lake. Or when he brings the invisible bird fluttering down in death, out of the high blue. "Hurt nothing unless you're forced to." And yet he lives by death, by killing the wild things of air and earth. But you have here the myth of the essential white American. All the other stuff, the love, the democracy, the floundering into lust, is a sort of by-play. The essential American soul is hard, isolate, stoic, and a killer. It has never yet melted.

—D. H. Lawrence, *Studies in Classic American Literature* (1922)

INTRODUCTION:
THE USES OF VIOLENCE

There is abroad in our land a diffusion of violence which appears to characterize American life and to reflect its very soul. So much does this violence pervade the contemporary American scene both on a social and on a private level that we are tempted to speak of the violent impulse in our national character. The American past, and her present, hardly challenge Lawrence's charge.

All of human history is borne on an unending and raging flood tide of violence. In one way or another, violence seems to be an ineradicable element in "human nature." Many behaviorists argue that at best it might take thousands of years to breed the aggressive instinct out of man even if we knew how to do it and had the will to do so.

But there is something in the American experience, in the American personality, soul, and culture, that makes this country at least appear to be more hyperactive to stress, more bloodthirsty in its response to frustration, than other societies. Ours has been a personality-violating culture since birth. We have been unable to resolve any of our greatest social and national problems without resort to violence. Again and again we have found it easier to crack skulls and spill blood in hot anger rather than apply the rule of reason or the yardstick of compromise.

Violence is a persisting pattern in the American social fabric. Progress in this country has not come about as a result of the honey-smooth flow of noble ideas translated into plausible law and acceptable custom by the gentle interaction of our constitutionally blessed executive, legislative, and judicial branches. Too often our history texts impress our young people with a grossly exaggerated image of the peacefulness with which change has been brought about in our land. The truth is that little of consequence has occurred in our history by executive fiat, legislative enactment, or judicial decision that has not had its violent precursor in an event or series of events which literally forced the issue. Somehow the hallowed principle has followed the violent fact.

Nor are the varieties of social violence in America— political, economic, and ethnic—mutually exclusive themes. Every episode of violence in the nation's history carried with it all three of these threads, although one strand usually appeared most prominently in any given event.

Take the theme of political violence, the lawlessness and violence growing out of politics and the relations of people to the government. This nation originated in an armed rebellion against the then established government. But economic as well as political grievances were very much a part of the picture. Indeed many historians argue that it was the economic conflict which led to revolt and not issues of political rights. And the new government which came to replace the "tyrannical" British crown found her constituents hardly any more tractable. The "little rebellions" almost affectionately recalled as Shays' Rebellion and the Whiskey Rebellion, led, respectively, by Massachusetts and Pennsylvania farmers against the new republic, reflected struggles against economic injustices as well as against perceived political oppression committed by the state and federal governments.

In modern times the violence which erupted on the campus of the University of Mississippi after a federal court order forced the admission of James Meredith, black, to the university is viewed as an episode of political violence because it presented a challenge to the political authority of the federal government—perhaps the first such kind since the Civil War. But something much more than politics was involved here. The white citizens of Oxford, Mississippi, were as much motivated by their perception of an economic threat from the educated black man and by their ethnic or racial hatred of all blacks as they were by their distaste for and distrust of a distant federal government which was threatening their personal lives through the "imposition" of a black presence.

The violence of the abolitionist movement in the mid-1800's can too readily be considered strictly ethnic in nature because the racial element was so obvious. But while the black man was indeed the subject of the conflict, the clashing parties were largely white on both sides of what was actually a political issue. The abolitionists themselves were not primarily concerned with economic or racial equality; political freedom was their essential objective. The antiabolitionists, on the other hand, were harboring fears not only of the black political threat but of the competition from free blacks in the labor market. Thus between the two contending sides all three strands of violence are evident.

By the same token, black-white "racial" violence, ranging from the slave insurrections of the first half of the nineteenth century through the urban ghetto riots of the 1960's, has been chiefly motivated by economic and political factors. The threat of economic and political competition, and thus of economic and political power, is the keystone of most black-white conflict, while the racial issue serves as a more obvious target of hate and fear.

The Draft Riots in 1863, resulting as they did in the brutal murder of some twelve hundred blacks in New York City alone over a period of days, was not simply a race riot. Less visible but no less present in the situation were the economic and political factors. The job threat from the black worker who was exempted from the draft law, and the resentment against fellow white citizens who could afford to purchase exemptions as provided by the law, drove the masses to kill blacks and destroy property belonging both to the affluent whites and the federal government.

Political as well as racial motives were behind the violence in the post-Civil War South. White men murdered black men to prevent them from using the ballot and thereby gaining political power. There was also evidence of economic motives in the lynchings. The frequency of lynchings varied inversely with indices of better economic conditions after the close of Reconstruction from 1882 through 1930. The savage violence which bloodied the Southern scene surely reflected naked racial hatred, but it was spawned by economic and political considerations.

Ethnic violence in American history was directed at groups other than the black people, and in such cases politics or economics or both were again factors in the situation.

It is true that many white Americans regarded the Indian as an inferior because of his red color alone; killing one evoked no more remorse than killing a buck in the wilderness. But the Indian murders were also part of the process of expropriating the red man's lands. Recourse to violence was habitual when Manifest Destiny was frustrated by an "unreasonable" people along America's frontiers. Of course extermination of the Indians to further American expansionism was not a stated government policy as was, for example, the "legitimate" military aggression against Mexico in 1846–48. Still, political and economic factors caused the "unofficial" massacres carried out by government troops. While such troops and their leaders were often acting beyond government orders, expressing personal ethnic hatred, they were also carrying out a violent tradition already a part of the national past.

The massacres of Chinese mining and railroad workers which is part of the history of the American Far West in the second half of the nineteenth century evidenced contempt toward the yellow race, but it also reflected resentment toward the Chinese as workers who competed against the native whites in the labor market.

Religious groups, too, were victims of ethnic-based violence in America's history. Most of us are familiar enough with the earliest episodes of intolerance and violence which marked the fate of nonconforming religious sects during the earliest settlements on the American continent. Not so well known, however, are the attacks and rioting committed against the Irish-Catholics and the Mormons through a good part of the last century. Both groups were as much resented for their growing economic affluence and political influence as they were for their religious tenets, so that the violence committed against them was political and economic as well as ethnic.

In another arena, the violence of the American labor movement, which marked the working man's struggle for decent wages and humane working conditions, and the violence of the repressive response of management, represent violence unmatched by any other social conflict in our national past. The great railroad uprisings, the Homestead Strike, the Ludlow Massacre, the bloody confrontations which marked labor relations in the 1930's—these are but a fraction of the violent episodes which were legion in America's labor history. Political and ethnic factors played a role in what was ostensibly economic violence. The political ideas and ideals of foreign-born leaders as well as rank-and-file members had, for example, as much to do with the violence of the Haymarket Riot in Chicago as did the economic issues involved in the McCormick Harvester Company lockout and strike which triggered the incident. The predominantly immigrant workers involved in the great Lawrence, Massachusetts, strike made the ethnic factor a crucial element in the affair.

The violence of the American frontier in the settlement of the West also represented all three themes of social violence. Armed conflict between cattle ranchers and sheep grazers over rights to grass and water was no less an example of economic violence than the struggle between labor and management along the industrial frontier. The sorry work of the vigilante committees was a political act defying the political structure of the community and a denial of the civil liberties and civil rights of individuals. The quick kill of the Indian was ethnic violence at its worst, as was the murder of Mexicans, victims of frontier vigilante "justice." It is said that the life-and-death struggle with a raw continent put a low price tag on the existence of any single human being who stood in the way of the next man's ambition. Cruelty was often the price of survival, and every man set his own limits. This explanation of the origins of the violent strain in our national pathology must be viewed against the frontier societies of Canada and Australia, which never produced the level of violence that the American frontier did.

In retrospect it can be argued that the ultimate outcome of the use of violence has been the preservation rather than the destruction of the American political and economic system. A number of leading historians even contend that violence has been a necessary and useful element in helping that system endure. This is why, the theory goes, the far left today calls for all-out destruction, recognizing that for them the preservative quality of a little violence is counter-revolutionary. Psychologists have argued that violence is a shortcut toward gaining an objective; it stands at the very beginning of man's becoming a socialized human being. At least one noted sociologist postulates that in the wilderness of cities, just as in the wilderness of the frontier, the gun becomes an effective equalizer. His premise is that when all legitimate channels to achievement are barred, violence may offer an alternate road.

All this amounts to the rather benign view that within limits violence has a useful social purpose and is a part of our normal social functioning. The historical record shows that some social issues have been settled by violence.

But now we have moved into a time and place in our historical development which makes the positive social function of violence questionable. What Arthur Schlesinger has called our "national propensity toward violence" may yet lead to total self-destruction unless we acknowledge this impulse as destructive. As Freud states in his *Civilization and Its Discontents*, "The fateful question for the human species seems to me to be whether and to what extent their cultural development will succeed in mastering the disturbance of their communal life by the human instinct of aggression and self-destruction."

This chronicle of violence in the American experience shows that contemporary violence is part of a persisting tradition as well as a state of the human condition. The crucial issue is whether this society which has committed its resources to the conquest of space and is about to succeed in that achievement can successfully solve the vast problems confronting the community on earth without destroying itself. Given the lesson of the American past, the future does not augur well.

1

VIOLENCE ON THE INDIAN FRONTIER

*". . . they came to be thought
of as game to be shot . . ."*

Historians studying contemporary society will find that
fighting and killing mark a good deal of American literature. Literary treatments of violence have always reflected
certain historical conditions and circumstances. For example, genocide against the Indians is the theme of much
of nineteenth-century fiction.[1]

Following James Fenimore Cooper through countless
chases, escapes, and battles, one loses track of the bodies
of Indians and renegades strewn behind.

The convention of Indian-killing as a kind of rite of passage
goes back in American fiction at least to 1799, when Charles
Brockden Brown's Edgar Huntley overcomes religious scruples
and tomahawks an Indian in order to rescue a captive maiden.
By 1837 a father in Robert Montgomery Bird's immensely
popular *Nick of the Woods* can boast that his son had killed
his first "brute" at the age of 14, and had then "blubbered"
all night after realizing he might have killed two. Such tales

did not shock a reading public thoroughly familiar with the treachery and inhumanity of Indians, and convinced of the need for exterminating them as if they were poisonous reptiles. When we recall that for some two centuries Americans were engaged in a continuing racial war, it is not surprising that so much fictional violence should center on the red man. To kill an Indian was a ritual that sealed one's claim to the rights and privileges of the white man's civilization; it was a symbolic acknowledgment that American freedom and wealth depended on the aborigine's blood. While some "good" Indians were portrayed, the most faithful brave could not be assimilated into white society. He was always the last Mohican, the dying warrior whose self-sacrifice contributed in some vague way to a greater society.[2]

The historical veracity of fictional accounts of violence against the Indian can be easily demonstrated. Here, for example, are excerpts from a description by Benjamin Franklin of a massacre in 1764:

These Indians were the remains of a tribe of the Six Nations, settled at Conestogo, and thence called Conestogo Indians. On the first arrival of the English in Pennsylvania, messengers from this tribe came to welcome them, with presents of venison, corn, and skins; and the whole tribe entered into a treaty of friendship with the first proprietor, William Penn, which was to last "as long as the sun should shine, or the waters run in the rivers."

This treaty has been since frequently renewed, and the chain brightened, as they express it, from time to time. It has never been violated, on their part or ours, till now. . . .

It has always been observed that Indians settled in the neighbourhood of white people do not increase, but diminish continually. This tribe accordingly went on diminishing, till there remained in their town on the manor but twenty persons, viz., seven men, five women, and eight children, boys and girls. . . .

This little society continued the custom they had begun, when more numerous, of addressing every new governor, and every descendant of the first proprietor, welcoming him to the province, assuring him of their fidelity, and praying a continuance of that favor and protection they had hitherto experienced. They had accordingly sent up an address of this kind to our present governor, on his arrival; but the same was scarce delivered when the unfortunate catastrophe happened, which we are about to relate.

On Wednesday, the 14th of December, of 1763, fifty-seven men from some of our frontier townships, who had projected the destruction of this little commonwealth, came, all well mounted, and armed with fire-locks, hangers, and hatchets, having travelled through the country in the night, to Conestogo manor. There they surrounded the small village of Indian huts, and just at break of day broke into them all at once. Only three men, two women, and a young boy were found at home, the rest being out among the neighbouring white people, some to sell the baskets, brooms, and bowls they manufactured, and others on other occasions. These poor defenceless creatures were immediately fired upon, stabbed, and hatcheted to death! The good Shehaus, among the rest, cut to pieces in his bed. All of them were scalped and otherwise horribly mangled. Then their huts were set on fire, and most of them burnt down. Then the troop, pleased with their own conduct and bravery, but enraged that any of the poor Indians had escaped the massacre, rode off, and in small parties, by different roads, went home. . . . those cruel men again assembled themselves, and, hearing that the remaining fourteen Indians were in the workhouse at Lancaster, they suddenly appeared in that town, on the 27th of December. Fifty of them, armed as before, dismounting, went directly to the workhouse, and by violence broke open the door, and entered with the utmost fury in their countenances. When the poor wretches saw they had no protection nigh, nor could possibly escape, and being without the least weapon for defence, they divided into their little families, the children clinging to the parents; they fell on their knees, protested their innocence, declared their love to the English, and that in their whole lives they had never done them injury; and in this posture they all received the hatchet! Men, women, and little children were every one inhumanly murdered in cold blood!

The barbarous men who committed the atrocious fact, in defiance of government, of all laws human and divine, and to the eternal disgrace of their country and color, then mounted their horses, huzzahed in triumph, as if they had gained a victory, and rode off *unmolested*!

The bodies of the murdered were then brought out and exposed in the street, till a hole could be made in the earth to receive and cover them. But the wickedness cannot be covered; the guilt will lie on the whole land, till justice is done on the murderers. The blood of the innocent will cry to Heaven for vengeance. . . .

Another proclamation has been issued, offering a great reward for apprehending the murderers. . . .

These proclamations have as yet produced no discovery, the murderers having given out such threatenings against those that disapprove their proceedings, that the whole country seems to be in terror, and none dare speak what he knows; even the letters from thence are unsigned in which any dislike is expressed of the rioters. . . .[3]

But it was not only the first-generation settlers along the Atlantic seaboard who harbored hatred and struck with savage violence at the red natives in their own land. The violence of later generations of American settlers who by the 1850's had reached as far west as California and the Oregon Territory was perhaps the greatest witnessed on the continent. One of the early immigrants to Oregon,

John Beeson, portrays some of his fellow men of the over-romanticized covered-wagon epoch:

> The majority of the first Emigrations to Oregon were from Missouri, and among them it was customary to speak of the Indian as a buck; of the woman as a squaw; until, at length, in the general acceptance of these terms, they ceased to recognize the rights of Humanity in those to whom they were applied. By a very natural and easy transition, from being spoken of as brutes, they came to be thought of as game to be shot, or as vermin to be destroyed. . . .
>
> On [one] occasion, a white man being found dead, he was supposed to have been killed by Indians. A company was made up forthwith, an Indian ranch was surrounded, and all the inmates put to death, men, women, and children. The domineering spirit grew by what it fed on, until, excited to madness by these oft-recurring scenes of blood, men became utterly regardless of justice, even towards those of their own race. Whatever a man's private views might be, he was expected to go with the crowd, to the full extent of every enterprise, and the more questionable the object, the more did they insist that all should participate. Personal freedom was thus frequently invaded; and life itself was not secure. On one occasion, an aged white man who had persistently continued at his mining, and utterly refused to take part against the Indians, was visited by twenty men and forced to mount his pony, and go in pursuit. After resting on the mountains, they shot him, cut off his head, leaving it on the limb of a tree, and divided his property among themselves.[4]

While the Iroquois scalped and tortured prisoners before the whites came, the colonists' incentives and precedents were mostly responsible for spreading these brutal practices among the Indians of the West. It was Governor Kieft of the New Netherlands, predecessor of the better-

known but no less admirable Peter Stuyvesant, who offered
the first scalp bounties. He publicly offered ten fathoms of
wampum for each head of a Raritan Indian brought in
by anyone. In 1642 some of these local Indians killed a
Dutch farmer who had earlier killed an Indian woman
for stealing his peaches. They would not surrender the
taker of blood revenge to Kieft. About a year later, in
1643, Kieft and his council had a drunken party. A few
advocates of violence in the council at this affair persuaded
Kieft that now would be the right time to punish the river
Raritans for refusing to surrender the murderers of the
Dutch farmer the year before. A massacre was suggested
as a proper punishment and Kieft gave the order.[5]

After they had sobered up a bit, the men still thought
the plan was a good one, but Kieft himself had some second
thoughts. His councillors, however, assured him that his
doubt of God's approval of such a course was foolish, and
that "not only God but the opportunity should be taken
into consideration."

Kieft, praying that "our God may bless the expedition,"
sent off his councillors with an armed body of men in the
dead of night to attack the sleeping villagers.[6] Eighty
Indians were killed while they slept, and thirty were taken
prisoners. The heads of the murdered were brought back
to Manhattan as trophies.

An eyewitness, a settler named De Vries, described the
events surrounding the massacre:

> I remained that night at the governor's setting up. I went and
> sat in the kitchen, when, about midnight, I heard a great
> shrieking, and I ran to the ramparts of the fort, and looked

over to Pavonia. Saw nothing but firing, and heard the shrieks of the Indians murdered in their sleep. I returned again to the house by the fire. . . .

When it was day the soldiers returned to the fort, having massacred or murdered 80 Indians, and considering that they had done a deed of Roman valour, in murdering so many in their sleep; where infants were torn from their mothers' breasts and hacked to pieces in the presence of their parents and the pieces thrown into the fire and in the water, and other sucklings were bound to small boards and then cut, stuck, and pierced, and miserably massacred in a manner to move a heart of stone. Some were thrown into the river, and when the fathers and mothers endeavored to save them, the soldiers would not let them come on land but made both parents and children drown, children from five to six years of age, and also some decrepit persons. Many fled from this scene, and concealed themselves amid the neighboring sedge, and when it was morning, came out to beg a piece of bread, and to be permitted to warm themselves; but they were murdered in cold blood and tossed into the water. . . . Some came by our lands in the country with their hands, some with their legs cut off, and some holding their entrails in their arms, and others had such horrible cuts and gashes that worse than they were could not happen. . . . After this exploit the soldiers were rewarded for their services, and Director Kieft thanked them by taking them by the hand and congratulating them.[7]

At about the same time Kieft, despite the colonies' continued losses in Indian engagements, recommended "that to restore peace and quiet in the country the Indians who waged war on us should by force of arms be utterly destroyed and exterminated."[8] This may have been the first official statement of what later became an unstated but perhaps implicit policy of the American people if not of their government.

An extermination policy was, as a matter of fact, being pursued in many parts of the country throughout much of the nineteenth century. A General Ord, who was in command of the Department of California of the Military Division of the Pacific, was a particularly enthusiastic exterminator so far as the Apaches were concerned. He wrote in September, 1868:

> I encouraged the troops to capture and root out the Apache by every means, and to hunt them as they would wild animals. This they have done with unrelenting vigor. Since my last report over two hundred have been killed, generally by parties who have trailed them for days and weeks into the mountain recesses, over snows, among gorges and precipices, lying in wait for them by day, and following them by night . . . though we have lost quite a number of soldiers. I think the Apaches have discovered that they are getting the worst of it.[9]

The Indian wars of the Far West in the nineteenth century fill volumes. The Sand Creek Massacre in Colorado is characteristic of the violent incidents which were a part of this period in American history.

In Colorado, relations between the early settlers and the Indians, Cheyennes, had been strained from the start. Alarmed at the intrusion and hostility of the whites, Indian marauders had stolen horses and cattle, and had interrupted and destroyed the mails. They had attacked the caravans of emigrants and traders, plundering the wagons, driving off the horses and mules, and killing some of the whites; and they had cut off all supply roads between the Missouri River and Denver. The people of Denver were infuriated when the bodies of the four members of the

Huntgate family, mutilated and scalped, were drawn through the streets in an ox wagon and put on display.

There were further clashes between the two groups: Wolf-Coming-Out and Bull-Telling-Tales, after being attacked, killed a white officer; then troops wantonly shot down Chief Lean Bear as he rode forward alone to greet a company of Colorado Volunteers.

The formation of the Colorado Volunteers came as a result of the Civil War. The war had made Colorado's military defense inadequate, and punitive steps were taken by Territorial* troops to protect the settlers. The volunteers enlisted for short periods of service and elected their own officers. They were under no real supervision or discipline, and were, to all intents and purposes, simply irresponsible gangs of armed men wandering about the Plains. Indeed some of the men of military age preferred a brief enlistment in the Colorado Volunteers, fighting Indians on the home front, to conscription in the Union Army, fighting Johnny Reb in the East and South. Others were reluctant to leave their families unprotected. To such men an Indian war seemed little short of a personal necessity.

In June, 1864, Governor John Evans called on friendly Indians to camp near the forts so they would not be wiped out in the pending war of extermination. He had issued a proclamation calling on all able-bodied citizens of Colorado to take up arms, advising them to hunt down Indians and kill every warrior they found.

On the morning of November 29, 1864, Colonel J. M. Chivington, a Methodist preacher in civilian life and known as a ruthless character, arrived at Fort Lyon with

* Colorado had not yet attained statehood.

his volunteer troops numbering several hundreds. Fort Lyon was one of the forts Governor Evans promised would protect friendly tribes. On the basis of that promise, five tribes settled themselves within twenty-five miles of the fort. The volunteers were out for blood, and they did not care whether the Cheyennes in Black Kettle's Camp on Sand Creek were friendly or not. Their orders were to "take no prisoners," "to kill all, little and big." "The only good Indian is a dead Indian" was their motto.

Chivington had more than seven hundred men under his command. One of his guides was Jim Beckwourth, a black mountain man and noted in the history books as the discoverer of Beckwourth Pass in California's Rockies.

A Lieutenant James D. Connor of the New Mexico Volunteers testified about the attack before a Senate investigating committee which studied the massacre several months later:[10]

About daybreak on the morning of the 29th of November we came in sight of the camp of the friendly Indians aforementioned, and were ordered by Colonel Chivington to attack the same, which was accordingly done . . . the village of the Indians consisted of from one hundred to one hundred and thirty lodges, and, as far as I am able to judge, of from five hundred to six hundred souls, the majority of which were women and children; in going over the battleground the next day I did not see a body of man, woman, or child but was scalped, and in many instances their bodies were mutilated in the most horrible manner—men, women, and children's private parts cut out, etc.; I heard one man say that he had cut out a woman's private parts and had them for exhibition on a stick . . . according to the best of my knowledge and belief these atrocities that were committed were with the knowledge of J. M. Chivington, and I do not know of his taking any measures to prevent them; I heard of one instance of a child a few months old being thrown in the feed-box of a wagon, and after being carried some distance left on the ground to perish; I also heard of numerous instances in which men had cut out the private parts of females and stretched them over the saddle-bows, and wore them over their hats while riding in the ranks. . . .[11]

If this testimony is to be credited, then the notion that the use of Jewish flesh by the German Nazis for the making of lampshades was a unique practice is wrong; indeed when we detail some of the atrocities committed by white Americans against their black, yellow, and red fellow men, the reputation of the Nazis will not be so exclusive. What is different, however, is that at the very least our atrocities never reflected governmental sanction.

But to come back to the incident at hand, let us look at another officer's eyewitness account of the Sand Creek Massacre:

We arrived at the Indian village about daylight. . . . Colonel Chivington moved his regiment to the front, the Indians retreating up the creek, and hiding under the banks. . . . White Antelope ran towards our columns unarmed, and with both arms raised, but was killed. Several other of the warriors were killed in like manner. The women and children were huddled together, and most of our fire was concentrated on them. . . . The Indian warriors, about one hundred in number, fought desperately; there were about five hundred all told. I estimated the loss of the Indians to be from one hundred and twenty-five to one hundred and seventy-five killed; no wounded fell into our hands and all the dead were scalped. The Indian who was pointed out as White Antelope had his fingers cut off. Our force was so large that there was no necessity of firing on the Indians. They did not return the fire until after our troops had fired several rounds. . . . I told Colonel Chivington . . . that it would be murder, in every sense of the word, if he attacked these Indians. His reply was, bringing his fist down close to my face, "Damn any man who sympathizes with Indians." . . . he had come to kill Indians and believed it to be honorable to kill Indians under any and all circumstances.[12]

The Colorado Volunteers returned to Denver with their spoils of scalps and three terrified Indian children who were later exhibited in between acts at the local opera house. Once these atrocities were reported to the country, shock and even anger came from other parts of the nation. The Congressional investigating committee concluded after listening to testimony that Chivington

. . . deliberately planned and executed a foul and dastardly massacre, which would have disgraced the veriest savage among those who were victims of his cruelty. . . . It is difficult to believe that beings in the form of men, and disgracing the uniform of United States soldiers and officers, could commit or countenance the commission of such acts of cruelty and barbarity.[13]

Cooper's *Deerslayer* suggests that the violence which destroyed the American Indian was motivated by the desire to prove one's manhood and to win the esteem of one's fellow man.[14] Beyond this was the more ostensible objective of securing the safety of white settlers in their conquering of the American continent. The slaughter and extermination of the red man was perhaps the inevitable social process which takes place when two different cultural groups come into contact in the same geographic region and one of these cultures has the superior technology as well as the numbers to make its will prevail.

Of the three remaining social processes, viz., amalgamation, assimilation, or accommodation, the last was the most reasonable possibility. Here conflicting groups would settle their differences while retaining their separate identities. But both the need and the greed of the white man were too compelling, and extermination became the solution.

Whether the sacrifice of the Indian as a necessary act to achieve a "greater America" is testimony not so much to violence in the American character as it is to the limitations of man's vision at a particular stage of his culture is a question which may be answered in the coming resolution of white America's present conflict with his fellow black man. The possibility that this conflict will also be resolved by violence is real, however much remote. Historically, the record offers small hope.

NOTES

1. See David B. Davis, "Violence in American Literature," *Annals of the American Academy of Political and Social Science*, edited by Marvin Wolfgang, Vol. CCCLXIV (1966), pp. 28–36. The entire issue, under the title of "Patterns in Violence," is devoted to a provocative and perceptive group of articles on contemporary violence.
2. *Ibid.*, p. 32.
3. Benjamin Franklin, "A Narrative of the Late Massacres in Lancaster County of a Number of Indians, Friends of this Province, by Persons Unknown, with Some Observations on the Same," in John Bigelow, ed., *Works of Benjamin Franklin*, Vol. IV, Federal Edition (New York, 1904), pp. 22–48.
4. John Beeson, *A Plea for the Indians* (New York, 1858), pp. 16–21.
5. This account is drawn from William C. Macleod, *The American Indian Frontier* (New York, 1928), pp. 223–225.
6. For a fascinating discussion by Benjamin Franklin of the settlers' use of religion to justify the extermination of Indians, see Bigelow, *op. cit.*, p. 32: "With the Scriptures in their hands and mouths they can set at nought that express demand, *Thou shalt not murder,* and justify their wickedness by the command given Joshua to destroy the heathen. Horrid

perversion of Scripture and of religion! To father the worst of crimes on the God of peace and love!"

7. Quoted in Macleod, *op. cit.*, pp. 224–225.
8. *Ibid.*, p. 229.
9. Quoted in John P. Dunn, *Massacres of the Mountains* (London, 1856), p. 235.
10. See U.S. Senate, Reports of Committee, 39th Cong., 2d sess., Ser. 1279, Doc. No. 156 (1867).
11. *Ibid.*, pp. 53–74.
12. *Ibid.*, pp. 76–77.
13. *Ibid.*, p. 318.
14. See Davis, *op. cit.*, p. 26.

RACIAL VIOLENCE

". . . each eager to be the
first to light the fire . . ."

Violence between the black man and the white man is quickly and readily characterized as racial violence. While the racial element is real enough and certainly apparent, economics and politics are almost always in the background of the conflict. Even the earliest incidents of black-white violence, the uprisings of the black slaves against their white masters in the South, were interpreted as uprisings of an economic (servant) class or as political plots inspired by foreign agents rather than as uprisings of one race against another race.[1] As a matter of fact, whites were implicated in a slave plot in New York in 1741, and a white man and his family and a Catholic priest were executed.

The more intrenched the institution of slavery became in the South, the greater the fears Southern whites had about the reaction of blacks to their economic and political status as well as their social status. Before the end of the Colonial period the South had become an armed camp in which masters figuratively kept their guns cocked and trained on the slaves in order to keep them docile and tractable.

That the near obsession of many Southern whites with the possibility of recurrent slave revolts was warranted is evidenced by the many hundreds of uprisings which took place throughout the first half of the nineteenth century.[2] These slave revolts often reached the proportions of massacres. Most of the time, however, the blacks suffered the greatest number of deaths in the aftermath of revenge. The three major episodes of slave violence were the rebellions led by Gabriel Prosser, Denmark Vesey, and Nat Turner.

On September 1, 1800, eleven hundred slaves set out to destroy Richmond, Virginia. For months the blacks, led by a self-ordained preacher, Gabriel Prosser, planned the move, gathering swords, clubs, and almost anything else which could be used as weapons. The day before, August 31, over one thousand slaves met six miles outside of Richmond and began to march on the city, but a storm almost routed the insurgents. Two slaves had already informed the whites, and the governor had promptly called out more than six hundred troops and notified every militia commander in the state. Within days hundreds of slaves were arrested and at least thirty-five were executed. Prosser himself was captured in late September and was executed.

Probably the most elaborate if not the most successful insurrection of the period was the one led by Denmark Vesey in 1822. Vesey had bought his freedom for six hundred dollars in Charleston, South Carolina, in 1800.

Later he worked as a carpenter in the area and used his spare time to study the French Revolution and the successful slave revolts in Haiti. For a period of some twenty years he carefully plotted his revolt and chose his assistants. Together they made and collected their weapons: two hundred and fifty pike heads and bayonets, and three hundred daggers. Their aim was to seize Charleston. But Vesey, like Prosser, was betrayed by a slave who informed his master. At least 139 blacks were arrested, 47 of whom were executed, including Vesey.

The third major slave revolt of the nineteenth century was led by Nat Turner, a Southampton County, Virginia, slave. Turner was a mystic and his actions were based on a vision that he had been selected by God to lead the slaves against their white oppressors. He chose the Fourth of July, 1831, as the day, but when he became ill he postponed the revolt until he saw another sign. On August 13, when the sun turned a "peculiar greenish blue," he called the revolt for August 21. That night, leading a small band of slaves, he took as his first victims his master and the four members of the household. Taking arms and recruiting slaves as they went, the small group swelled into a well-armed band of seventy men. In quick succession other families fell before the blows of the blacks. Within twenty-four hours ten men, fourteen women, and thirty-five children were killed. The revolt was spreading rapidly when the main group of blacks were met and overpowered by the state and federal troops. More than one hundred slaves were killed in the encounter and thirteen slaves and three free blacks were immediately hanged. Turner was captured on October 30, and he was executed two weeks later.

The leading black historian, John Hope Franklin, has pointed out that slave revolts often included a number of whites who gave the blacks encouragement and assistance.[3] Whites in such cases were probably motivated by ideological principles as well as by perhaps their own economic plight caused by the existence of slave-labor competition. In any event, something more than race was involved in the "interracial" violence of the period.

The notorious and bloody Draft Riots in New York City in July, 1863, are also usually characterized as a major episode of racial violence in American history.[4] Yet economics and politics were very much a part of the background as well.

At the outset the Draft Riots were an insurrection against the political authority of the federal government. The violence was initially provoked by Congress's enactment of the Conscript and Enrollment Act. For this reason the first phase of the violence was directed against public officers and public buildings. In addition poor whites wanted to revenge themselves against the more affluent whites who could buy their way out of the draft by paying three hundred dollars for a substitute. And so the second phase of the rioting was directed against the brownstone houses of the well-to-do in the city. There was the further resentment against fighting a war "to free the niggers" and the fear that blacks would get the jobs whites would have to leave in order to fight. Throughout the rioting violence against blacks was part of the picture. According to *The New York Times*, "The worst feature of the riotous demonstrations . . . is the dastardly and wanton outrages upon the persons of our colored people."[5]

Again, the riots started as an insurrection against the United States government on a hot, sultry Monday morning, July 13.

The initiation of the draft on Saturday in the 9th Congressional district was characterized by so much order and good feeling as to well nigh dispel the forebodings of tumult and violence which many entertained in connection with the enforcement of conscription in this City. Very few, then, were prepared for the riotous demonstrations which yesterday from 10 in the morning until late last night prevailed almost unchecked in our streets. The authorities had counted upon more or less resistance to this measure of the Government after the draft was completed, and the conscripts were required to take their place in the ranks, and at that time they would have been fully prepared to meet it; but no one anticipated resistance at so early a stage in the execution of the law and consequently, both the City and National authorities were totally unprepared to meet it.

. . . Scarcely had two dozen names been called, when a crowd numbering perhaps 500, suddenly made an eruption in front of the (draft office) building (corner of 46th Street and 3rd Avenue) attacking it with clubs, stones, brickbats and other missiles. The upper part of the building was occupied by families, who were terrified beyond measure at the smashing of the windows, doors and furniture. Following these missiles, the mob rushed furiously into the office on the first floor, where the draft was going on, seizing the books, records, etc., all of which they destroyed, except those contained in an iron safe. The drafting officers were set upon with stones and clubs, and with the Reporters for the Press and others, had to make a hasty exit through the rear. They did not escape scatheless, however, as one of the enrolling officers was struck a savage blow with a stone, which will probably result fatally, and several others were injured. . . .

Soon after the rioting began Superintendent of Police Kennedy hurried to the scene in a carriage, and, as he alighted, a portion of the crowd recognized him, greeting him at first with uncomplimentary epithets and afterwards with blows. A score or more of the ruffians fell upon him, and dealt heavy blows upon his head, face, and body, injuring him severely. They doubtless would have killed him outright had not a strapping fellow in the crowd felt some compunction at the brutality of the rest and dashed into the rescue. . . .[6]

Once the mob had destroyed the draft machinery, its fury continued undiminished. Part of the crowd moved south on Third Avenue and headed for a four-story building on Second Avenue and Twenty-first Street which housed a gun factory with a state armory on the top floor. Police armed with night sticks, revolvers, and carbines had already taken positions at the doors and windows. Thousands of men and women were packed in the surrounding streets, hurling bricks and paving stones, firing pistols and muskets.

One group managed to break down a panel of the entrance door. The first to crawl through was killed instantly. Enraged at the sight of the victim's headless and bloody body, the mob came on again with sledges and crowbars, and formed human battering rams with telephone poles. The police inside escaped through a rear smoke exhaust pipe.

When the doors gave way, the rioters swarmed on the various floors, a few making their way to the top-floor drill room to seize the precious carbines and ammunition stored there. From every window of the building carbines were thrown to those waiting below. Others formed a human chain along which the guns were passed out to the street.

Fire broke out in several places in the building, probably set by rioters to prevent those inside from being arrested. Looters on the top floor were trapped by the flames and many of them either leaped to their deaths or were consumed by the flames. In the twenty-four-hour period of the attack, twenty-five rioters were known to have been killed and at least a hundred seriously wounded.

On other days of the rioting the mobs burned down public buildings such as police precincts, burned the homes of public officials, including the postmaster's home, and besieged the mayor's residence. These were politically motivated acts of violence.

Passing through a district of new and elegant brownstone houses, the mobs attacked and looted the buildings from cellar to roof. These were the homes of the rich, who could afford to buy their way out of the draft.

Racial violence prevailed throughout this many-faceted riot from the very outset to the last lingering hours when the riot finally subsided. One day's news account indicates the unmitigated cruelty and irrationality of the whites toward the black man:

> Among the most cowardly features of the riot and one which indicated its political *animus*, and the cunningly-devised cue that had been given to the rioters by the instigators of the outbreak, was the causeless and inhuman treatment of the negroes of the City. It seemed to be an understanding through-

out the City that the negroes should be attacked wherever
found, whether they offered provocation or not; as soon as
one of these unfortunate people was spied, whether on a cart,
a railroad car, or in the street, he was immediately set upon
by a crowd of men and boys, and unless some man of pluck
came to his rescue, or he was fortunate enough to escape into
a building, he was inhumanly beaten and perhaps killed. There
were probably not less than a dozen negroes beaten to death
in different parts of the City during the day. Among the most
diabolical of these outrages that have come to our knowledge is
that of a negro cartman living in Carmine street. About
eight o'clock in the evening as he was coming out of the stable,
after having put up his horses, he was attacked by a crowd
of about 400 men and boys, who beat him with clubs and
paving stones till he was lifeless; hung him to a tree opposite
the burying ground. Not being satisfied with their devilish
work, they set fire to his clothes and danced and yelled and
swore their horrid oaths around his burning corpse. The
charred body of the poor victim was still hanging upon the
tree at a late hour last evening. . . .[7]

The Draft Riots in New York probably resulted in the
greatest amount of bloodshed for both whites and blacks
in American history. Estimates of deaths of white rioters
alone range as high as 1,500, and while the total number
of blacks killed is unknown, the black population in the
city dropped by twenty percent, from 12,472 to 9,945,
between 1860 and 1865. Since a major factor in the origin
of these riots was a fear of black labor competition, they
might be properly described as an expression of racial
violence. But the basic economic and political overtones
must be borne in mind in this as well as in the other
episodes of violence involving blacks.

The years of Reconstruction in the South which followed
the Civil War were filled with an extraordinary amount of
atrocities, deprivations of rights, and every other kind of
abusive and illegal treatment of blacks.[8] Major General
Joseph A. Mower, Sheridan's successor in Louisiana, in
March, 1867, sent in a report on outrages in that state
from the beginning of the Freedmen's Bureau through
February 20, 1867. He gave a detailed account of seventy
murders of freed men by whites, suggesting that the number might have been twice that. He also described two
hundred and ten cases of whippings, beatings, and stab-
bings, and noted that in almost every instance the persons
guilty of these offenses had not been apprehended. The
records of the Bureau revealed a high degree of lawlessness
in almost all sections of the South.

In no other aspect was the effect of Reconstruction more
marked than in the area of violence. Racial feeling had
had nothing to do with the tendency to mob action in the
Old South. So long as the black man had been property,
worth from five hundred and fifty dollars up, he had been
safe from rope and whip more than any common white
man and maybe even safer than his master himself. But
with the abolition of legal slavery his immunity vanished.
It was in the economic interest of his former protectors,
that master class, to disabuse him of any illusion that his
liberty was real, and to confirm him in his ancient docility.
Now the way was open for the racial hate and cruel itch,
which for so long had been festering impotently in the
poor whites, to take the black in hand.[9]

The Ku Klux Klan originally was organized during
Reconstruction for the purpose of trying to control the

conduct of former slaves as well as for the very clear purpose of restoring the political power of the Old South.[10] Political murders were part of an extensive campaign of intimidation. Confessed members avowed that the Klan aimed at the prevention of black voting and the disruption of the federal government's programs to assist the freed men.

The work of the Klan in South Carolina was typical. It first appeared in the midst of the Grant-Seymour Presidential election campaign, in which control of the national administration as well as local offices were at stake. The Klan tried to create an atmosphere of terror in which black voters would be eliminated and victory in a crucial contest thereby assured for the Democrats. Murder was used as a weapon by the Klan. At least eight blacks were killed in incidents ranging across three countries. Among these was the murder of Randolph, a Presbyterian minister who had previously served as an assistant superintendent of education under the Freedmen's Bureau, and who was a member of the state senate from Orangeburg County. A Democratic leader in the state urged the Democrats "never to suffer this man Randolph to come in your midst; if he does, give him four feet by six."

The violence of the 1868 campaign reached a peak on Election Day. Extensive use of force was made to keep blacks away from the polls. Groups of armed whites drove blacks away from polling places, and in one county two blacks were killed outright.

The Klan expressed a deep-rooted American social habit, a habit of ready violence in defense of a threatened social and political status. Its ugly work has plagued the country in varying degrees from the late nineteenth century right down to the present day. If it were indeed "un-American," it would never have taken hold as it had and has.

But the violent impulse in the South is seen most clearly and dramatically in her preeminence in lynching. During the period of slavery, lynching was comparatively rare in the South. The Civil War, with its economic and political disruption combined with race hatred, extended the practice.

A report of the Southern Commission on the Study of Lynching gives the following description of a "typical" mob slaying:

> The sheriff along with the accused Negro was seized by the mob, and the two were carried to the scene of the crime. Here quickly assembled a thousand or more men, women, and children. The accused Negro was hung up in a sweet-gum tree by his arms, just high enough to keep his feet off the ground. Members of the mob tortured him for more than an hour. A pole was jabbed in his mouth. His toes were cut off, joint by joint. His fingers were similarly removed, and members of the mob extracted his teeth with wire pliers. After further unmentionable mutilations, the Negro's still-living body was saturated with gasoline and a lighted match was applied. As the flames leaped up, hundreds of shots were fired into the dying victim. During the day, thousands of people came from miles around to see the sight. Not until nightfall did the officers remove the body and bury it.[11]

By the late nineteenth century lynching became an expression of racial violence in the South. Most of those lynched, of course, were blacks, although a substantial number of whites were victims of lynch mobs, especially in the early period. The record by states, 1892–1945, showed no lynchings in New England. The Middle Atlantic, Midwestern, and most of the Western states ranked next with not more than fifty lynchings. The border states of Oklahoma, Missouri, and Kentucky ranked with the Southern States of Arkansas, Florida, South Carolina, and Tennessee with one hundred to three hundred lynchings. The worst record—more than three hundred lynchings—was shared by the remaining southern states: Alabama, Georgia, Louisiana, Mississippi, and Texas. At the end of 1956 Tuskegee Institute reported a seventy-five-year total of 4,733 lynchings in the United States. The eleven former states of the Confederacy accounted for 3,514—all but 490 of whom were blacks—nearly three times as many as in the remaining states combined.[12]

In any case, the first decade of the twentieth century was a peak decade for lynching in the South, while during the same period this pattern of racial violence spread into the Northern states. Many if not most lynchings expanded into full-scale riots carried out by whites against the local black community. One such episode took place in 1908 in Springfield, Ohio, where mobs gathered and broke into a jail where a black man was being held on charge of killing a police officer in an altercation. The white citizens murdered the black man in the doorway of the jail, hanged him to a telegraph pole, and riddled his body with bullets. They then proceeded to destroy the black ghetto of the town.[13]

One of the most spectacular lynchings of this century took place in Waco, Texas, 1916. Jesse Washington, a seventeen-year-old illiterate and slightly retarded farm hand was charged with the murder of a white woman. As the judge began writing in his docket the jury's guilty verdict,

A big fellow in the back of the courtroom yelled, "Get the Nigger!"

[The mob] dragged the boy down the stairs, put a chain around his body and hitched it to an automobile. The chain broke. The big fellow took the chain off the Negro under the cover of the crowd and wound it around his own wrist, so that the crowd [was] jerking at the man's wrist and he was holding the boy. The boy shrieked and struggled.[14]

The full report of an investigator for the NAACP who was sent from the New York office to Waco offers details so horrid and grotesque that most readers would not accept its truthfulness because of the source. Another account, in the local press, the Waco *Times-Herald*, presents a picture close enough to the details in the NAACP report to prove its reliability.

Great masses of humanity flew as swiftly as possible through the streets of the city in order to be present at the bridge when the hanging took place, but when it was learned that the Negro was being taken to the City Hall, crowds of men, women, and children turned and hastened to the lawn. On the way to the scene of the burning people on every hand took a hand in showing their feelings in the matter of striking the Negro with anything obtainable; some struck him with shovels, bricks, clubs, and others stabbed him and cut him until when he was strung up his body was a solid color of red; the blood of the many wounds inflicted covered him from head to foot.
Dry goods boxes and all kinds of inflammable material

were gathered, and it required but an instant to convert this into seething flames. When the Negro was first hoisted into the air his tongue protruded from his mouth and his face was besmeared with blood.

Life was not extinct within the Negro's body, although nearly so, when another chain was placed around his neck and thrown over the limb of a tree on the lawn, everybody trying to get to the Negro and have some part in his death. The infuriated mob then leaned the Negro, who was half alive and half dead, against the tree, he having just strength enough within his limbs to support him[self]. As rapidly as possible the Negro was then jerked into the air at which a shout from thousands of throats went up on the morning air and dry goods boxes, excelsior, wood and every other article that would burn was then in evidence, appearing as if by magic. A huge dry goods box was then produced and filled to the top with all of the material that had been secured. The Negro's body was swaying in the air, and all of the time a noise as of thousands was heard and the Negro's body was lowered into the box.

No sooner had his body touched the box than people pressed forward, each eager to be the first to light the fire; matches were touched to the inflammable material and as smoke rapidly rose in the air, such a demonstration as of people gone mad was never heard before. Everybody pressed closer to get souvenirs of the affair. When they had finished with the Negro boy his body was mutilated. Fingers, ears, pieces of clothing, toes and other parts of his body were cut off by members of the mob that had crowded to the scene as if by magic when the word that the Negro had been taken in charge by the mob was heralded over the city. . . .

Onlookers were hanging from the windows of the City Hall and every other building that commanded a sight of the burning, and as the Negro's body commenced to burn, shouts of delight went up from the thousands of throats and apparently everybody demonstrated in some way their satisfaction at the retribution that was being visited upon the perpetrator of such a horrible crime, the worst in the annals of McLennan county's history.

The body of the Negro was burned to a crisp, and was left for some time in the smouldering remains of the fire. Women and children who desired to view the scene were allowed to do so, the crowds parting to let them look on the scene. After some time the body of the Negro was jerked into the air where everybody could view the remains, and a mighty shout rose on the air.

While the torso of the boy was being dragged through the streets behind the horse, the limbs dropped off and the head was put on the stoop of a disreputable woman in the reservation district. Some little boys pulled out the teeth and sold them to some men for five dollars apiece. The chain was sold for twenty-five cents a link.

From the pictures, the boy was apparently a wonderfully built boy. The torso was taken to Robinson, hung to a tree, and shown off for a while, then they took it down again and dragged it back to town and put it on the fire again at five o'clock.[15]

Horrible as this episode was, it did not shock the nation into putting an end to "this modern barbarity."[16] Lynchings equally as primitive and brutal continued to take place not only in the South but in the North as well. In the Midwest, Omaha, Nebraska, a young black man who had been accused of raping a white girl was torn from his cell within hours after his arrest by a mob of whites who shot him and then hanged him from a nearby lamppost in September, 1919. His body was then burned and hung from a trolley pole at a major downtown intersection.[17]

Along with the pattern of lynching, mob assaults by whites against blacks was also a marked expression of the violence in the early part of the twentieth century. While charges of black assaults on white women were usually the triggering incident for the violence that followed, so that again it would seem to be a matter of racial violence in these events, economic and political factors were always somewhere in the background. Suppression of economic competition of political power was often as much of an objective of the violence as the aim to protect white woman-hood. This was particularly true in the South. The riots which occurred in Washington, D.C., in 1919, and in Tulsa, Oklahoma, in 1921, were examples of this.

Relations between the races in the capital had been affected by the accession of the Southern-oriented Wilson administration and by the World War. Beginning in 1913, blacks in the federal service had been segregated at work (where they had never been segregated before) by their new Southern supervisors, and there had been stirrings of anger among Washington's blacks over the suddenly more "Southern outlook of their lives. In addition to this, Washington's population had grown during the war by a large influx of Southern whites and a smaller influx of Southern blacks. The one group still aimed to "teach any fresh nigger his place," and the other determined to be free or win revenge—both of which swelled the racial tensions within the city.

These existing conflicts were brought to a boil by sen-sationalism in the press. In the summer of 1919 the local *Washington Post* carried on a campaign of criticism of the police for not controlling a "crime wave" of assaults. The usual summer crime statistics were played up as were ordinary cases of assault. Alleged instances of attempts by blacks to rape white women were given special prominence.

On July 9 the Washington branch of the NAACP sent a letter to all four daily newspapers in the city, "calling their attention to the fact that they were sowing the seeds of a race riot by their inflammatory headlines." Nevertheless the pattern continued. On July 19 the *Post* headlined a story, "NEGROES ATTACK GIRL . . . WHITE MEN VAINLY PURSUE." The girl "attacked" was the wife of a man in the naval aviation department. Two hundred sailors and marines decided to avenge the slight to his and their honor by lynching two black men who had been suspected of the attack but released by the police. The sailors moved into southwest Washington, stopping every black person they met and beating several, both men and women. District and military police responded to a riot call and dispersed the mob. Ten arrests were made: two white Navy men and eight blacks. When three more blacks were later stopped on the street by District police patrolling the area, one of them fired at the policemen and wounded them. This was the first use of violence by blacks, although the eight-to-two arrest ratio might indicate a higher rate of lawbreaking by blacks.

Sunday night the situation exploded. At about 10 P.M. a policeman arrested a young black man on a minor charge at a busy intersection on Pennsylvania Avenue, halfway between the Capitol and the White House. While the policeman waited for the patrol wagon, "hundreds of men in khaki and blue and many negroes" crowded around. The arrested black man was snatched away from the police by several white men and beaten over the head.

The police recovered him and dispersed the crowd, but arrested no whites. Down the street, a few minutes later, another fight broke out between white servicemen and black civilians.

From then on, the violence multiplied. Soldiers and sailors marched up Pennsylvania Avenue, chasing and beating blacks, yanking them off streetcars and growing increasingly more belligerent. Violent clashes continued through most of the night between civilians after the soldiers and sailors had returned to their barracks at midnight.

Throughout the day on Monday a flurry of meetings was held and statements issued on Sunday night's violence. During the afternoon, blacks, aroused by a *Post* news story that "a mobilization of every available service man stationed in or near Washington or on leave here has been ordered for tomorrow evening . . . The hour of assembly is nine o'clock and the purpose is a 'clean up' that will cause the events of the last two evenings to pale into significance," began to arm themselves. Guns were bought in Washington and Baltimore. "Alley Negroes," some of them soldiers from the black regiment recruited in Washington, took out the rifles they had used in France. During the day came the first evidence of the blacks' determination to fight back and even to attack. One mob of twenty-five or thirty boarded a streetcar and beat the motorman and conductors. Others fired from a speeding automobile at sailors on the Naval Hospital grounds.

That night the riot was renewed with greater violence than the night before. Four men were killed outright and dozens were seriously wounded.

The force that had been set up to cope with the riots was made up of seven hundred Washington police and four hundred soldiers, sailors, and marines organized as an emergency provost guard. Few servicemen took part in the Monday night disturbances. But a surging mob of one thousand white civilians made repeated attempts to break through a cavalry cordon in order to attack the black residential sections. Several cavalry charges broke up these attempts. Whenever the mob found blacks in the downtown area, they beat them savagely. Police were able to keep the mob moving but not to disperse it. Some blacks caught in the melee responded to the attack by firing pistols at the mob.

Meanwhile in the black areas blacks were beating white men and were firing upon passing streetcars and autos from houses along the way. Eight or ten automobiles manned by armed black men were used as armored cavalry in lightning attacks on white residential districts, randomly firing at houses and people. Other automobiles were used by whites in the same fashion, and at least one running dogfight was reported between blacks and whites in two such cars. Several policemen were wounded or killed while trying to arrest armed blacks or to raid houses that had been used as sniper centers.

On Tuesday the press was calling for martial law. But the District commissioners rejected this and worked out plans for more military support of the civil government. By nightfall, the combined factors of two thousand federal troops, admonitions for self-control from the NAACP to the black community, and an intermittent driving rain together succeeded in preventing crowds from gathering. By Wednesday night the four days of rioting subsided.

The analysis of the Washington riots led to the conclusion that the blacks were now going to protect themselves whenever they felt unprotected by the law. It was the conclusion of both the black community and a number of white newspapers outside Washington that the Washington police had acted with partiality rather than with neutrality.[18]

Two years later, in 1921, Tulsa, Oklahoma, offered the nation a second "Southern style" race riot. In the months and weeks immediately before the outbreak of violence, the city as well as the state as a whole had experienced a steady deterioration of race relations. White Oklahomans, like whites in other parts of the South and North, had been upset at the new attitudes which many blacks brought back to the United States after service in the military forces overseas. Within the country the war had brought about increased black demands for equal rights and opportunities due them as citizens. Oklahoma was, in 1921, experiencing a minor agricultural recession. Many rural Northerners had been moving into urban centers. Furthermore, it was believed that agitators, particularly the Industrial Workers of the World (IWW) and "bolshevik" organizers, plus African nationalist groups which were just beginning to grow at that time, were contributing to the disaffection of the black community.

When news reached them that a black man had been accused of assaulting a young white woman, blacks took arms to the jail to protect the accused, who, it was rumored, would be lynched. Excerpts from *The New York Times* reporter offer a vivid picture of the events which followed:

After twenty-four hours one of the most disastrous race wars encountered upon an American city, during which time eighty-five or more persons were killed and the negro quarter of Tulsa, comprising upward of thirty densely populated blocks, was wiped out by fire, the State militia had gained virtual control tonight and the rioting seems to have come to an end.

An official estimate early tonight was eighty-five dead of whom it was said twenty-five might be whites and sixty negroes. This followed a statement issued by Police Chief Daly, saying that he believed the probable ultimate loss to be 175, and that many persons lost their lives in fires. Late tonight, however, the known dead were seventy-seven, of whom nine were white and sixty-eight negroes. One hundred whites and two hundred negroes were estimated to have been wounded seriously. All the local hospitals are filled to overflowing, and emergency relief has been started by the Red Cross, YMHA, YWCA, and other welfare organizations.

The entire "black belt" of Tulsa is now only a smoldering heap of blackened ruins. Hardly a negro shanty is standing throughout an area that housed upward [of] 150,000 blacks. Domesticated animals wandering among the wreckage give the only token of life over a desolate territory, extending from the Frisco tracks to Sand Pipe Hill on the north. Looting by lawless elements goes on sporadically.

Tulsa city and Tulsa county are under martial law, proclaimed at noon. Ordinances, promulgated by the military authorities, who are in charge of the city, established a curfew at 7 o'clock this evening and no person, white or black, was allowed abroad after that hour without credentials.

State Guardsmen with fixed bayonets patrol all the streets of the business and railroad districts, and armed police and automobiles move through the city to break up suspicious gatherings.

THE BATTLE OF WASHITA: THE ATTACK ON BLACK KETTLE'S
CHEYENNE CAMP BY THE SEVENTH REGIMENT CAVALRY UNDER
MAJOR-GENERAL GEORGE A. CUSTER

LYNCHING: TEMPLE, TEXAS, 1917

LYNCH MOB CREMATING BLACK
YOUTH IN OMAHA, NEBRASKA, 1919

OF THE KU KLUX KLAN,
19TH CENTURY

ABOLITIONIST VIOLENCE: THE DESTRUCTION
OF LOVEJOY'S PRINTING PRESS

Brown Brothers

DRAFT RIOTS IN NEW YORK CITY, 1863

Culver Pictures

THE MOBBING OF WILLIAM LLOYD GARRISON, 1835

ANDREW OLIVER, STAMP COLLECTOR,
ATTACKED BY THE MOB

THE WHISKEY REBELLION, 1792

Brown Brothers

DESTRUCTION OF TEA IN BOSTON HARBOR

ANTI-CATHOLIC RIOTS IN PHILADELPHIA, 1844

MOUNTAIN MEADOWS MASSACRE: 132 EMIGRANTS KILLED BY MORMONS AND INDIANS

MASSACRE OF MORMONS AT HAUN'S MILL

ANTI-CHINESE RIOTS

OUT WEST WHERE THEY HUNG ENTIRE JURY OF
12 MEN BECAUSE THEIR DECISION HAD BEEN "BOUGHT"

THE GREAT RAILROAD STRIKE/FIGHT AT HARPERSVILLE, N.Y., 1877

BALTIMORE & OHIO STRIKE, AUGUST, 1877

WORKERS DEFY PICKETS AT
FORD PLANT IN DEARBORN, 1941

Brown Brot

HUNGER STRIKERS STORMING
FORD PLANT IN DEARBORN, MICHIGAN, 1932

Six thousand negroes are under heavy guard in hastily established detention camps. Most of these are at the baseball parks.

The race war that resulted in such a tragedy developed with great speed. . . .

The police were unable to control the situation. Every hardware and sporting goods store in the city was broken into as the fast assembling whites armed themselves.

Soon automobile skirmish parties appeared and through the night the machines sped through the streets bristling with rifles and shotguns. At midnight the negro army before the courthouse began to disintegrate, the negroes filtering back through side streets of their home district. Here, heavily entrenched, they held the whites at bay until daybreak.

As soon as dawn came 500 whites began the invasion of the negro quarter. Sharp fighting occurred in the railroad and freight yards, the whites steadily gaining ground as their numbers increased. Negro snipers maintained a harrassing fire from windows and housetops.

Fires had been started by the white invaders soon after 1 o'clock and other fires were set from time to time. By 8 o'clock practically the entire thirty blocks of homes in the negro quarters were in flames and few buildings escaped destruction. Negroes caught in their burning homes were in many instances shot down as they attempted to escape.

Heavy damage is reported to have been done property in the freight districts. The Frisco Railroad suffered considerable loss. . . .

The first shooting affray came soon after dark, when a negro was stopped by a police officer and his gun taken away. He attempted to resist, according to the officer, and was shot dead.

The heaviest fighting was in the northern section, where hundreds of negroes were concentrated in a valley. Fifty were barricaded in a church.

Several massed attacks were launched against the church, but each time the attackers had to fall back under the heavy fire of the negro defenders. Finally a torch was applied to the building and the occupants began to pour out, firing as they ran. Several of the negroes were killed.

At noon the Fire Chief, speaking of the continued spread of flames, said:

"We can't use the equipment we have, and for that reason we have not asked for more apparatus from other cities. It would mean a fireman's life to turn a stream of water on one of those negro buildings. They shot at us all morning when we're trying to do something, but none of my men were hit. There is not a chance in the world to get through that mob into the negro district."

There was a tendency to blame the police force and the sheriff's office. As Adjt. General Charles J. Barrett, who is military dictator of the city, put it:

"If those first armed negroes had been summarily arrested or, refusing to yield, had been shot on the spot, this blot of disgrace would not now rest upon your city."[19]

The Chicago race riot of 1919 perhaps best exemplified the "Northern style" urban race riot.[20] Here, neither the background cause nor the precipitating incident was at all related to an alleged violation of the sanctity of white womanhood, which so characterized Southern riots. Instead there was a long period of increasing tensions which challenged the economic, social, and political structures imposed upon the blacks by the white power structure. The challenge was felt particularly in the areas of housing, labor, and the use of public facilities, especially transportation.

The situation in Chicago in July, 1919, can be summarized briefly. Nationally there was general concern over postwar economic adjustments, and more particularly over the role of unions and of blacks in the postwar labor force. Locally the atmosphere reflected national tensions. There had been quarrels and eruptions of violence over housing, recreation, and transportation. There had been bombings and interracial assaults (including the murder of two blacks by white gangs). And the previous spring, signs had appeared warning the people that "We're going to get the niggers on July 4th." Efforts had increased to prevent this, and there was no eruption of violence on that date. But Chicago was ripe for social violence, and a riot was just around the corner.

On July 27, 1919, large crowds of blacks and whites were bathing on the beach at Twenty-ninth Street and Lake Michigan. It was a hot Sunday following a hot and sultry summer week. As in the past, an unseen line divided the two groups, and blacks and whites kept to their own sides of the division. This particular afternoon a black youth slipped across the line and climbed onto a raft in the "white" section. Rocks were thrown, and whatever the sequence of actual events might have been, the black youth was drowned. (A coroner's jury ruled he died of drowning because he was afraid to swim in to the shore.) After this incident blacks and whites joined in the diving for the body. As the crowds increased, demands were made that the boys who had been throwing the stones be arrested. The policeman on duty refused. It was at this point that the first violence between blacks and whites occurred, in the form of jostling and exchanging insults. Then, in this already rumor-rife situation, a black man was arrested, by the same policeman, on the complaint of a white man. Blacks attacked the policeman. The Chicago race riot had started.

Rioting that ended in looting, larson and murder broke loose in Chicago's "black belt" tonight. It was the most serious race rioting that has ever stained the history of Illinois. Before midnight, fourteen had been killed and seventy-six injured. Of the dead nine were white. Twenty-nine white persons were hurt and forty-seven negroes.

The disorder which had been going on all day, grew serious at night with the hurling of bricks and the firing of revolvers at 35th Street and Wabash Avenue at 7:30 P.M. Before many hours had passed the outbreaks had spread to the Stock Yards district, to 35th and Halstead Streets all through the "black belt" and into the Hyde Park district. Every available policeman in the city was rushed to the scene; former soldiers and sailors were sworn into the National Guard and the reserve militia regiments had been called out and were being mobilized; the hospitals were crowded with victims; the street cars and the elevated trains had ceased to run on the South Side; telephone wires were cut; scores of white men and black were under arrest.

The fighting at 35th Street was the fiercest of the early evening. Here five negroes were killed and scores wounded, two policemen were wounded, one of them after he had made a barricade of his horse and fought Indian fashion, from the cover of his mount.

General Dickinson said he would remain in Chicago in charge of the military situation. He pointed out that the 11th Infantry and the 1st Reserve Regiments have machine gun companies with experienced machine gunners, and that the line companies of these two regiments are armed with new Springfield rifles and Krag-Jorgensen carbines.

"They all have plenty of ammunition," said General Dickinson, "and if all the race rioters on the South Side were to combine, the militiamen would be able to handle the situation."

One report was that the South Side colored men have 1500 Springfield rifles of the type formerly used by the Government and placed on sale throughout the city in department stores after their condemnation for Government use. This was denied by colored Aldermen, but was admitted by many of the negroes [who] possessed arms of one kind or another and were prepared to defend themselves against aggression. The chief fear expressed was that the young hotheads might organize and start a general uprising.

Early in the afternoon white men gathered in groups and stoned, stabbed or shot at lone colored men wherever they appeared. The negroes in retaliation formed gangs and began to stab, shoot and throw missiles at automobiles, street cars or wagons containing white men, and to attack those on the street who were not under actual protection of the police.

Groups of blacks formed in football fashion and charged against whites with razors and clubs. On one corner the scene was like a miniature battleground. Unconscious negroes and whites dotted the street. As they regained consciousness they were arrested or permitted to leave the neighborhood.

In one fracas on 34th Street negroes knocked two policemen unconscious and were drawing pistols when a group of discharged negro soldiers came to the rescue of the whites. . . .

Whenever negroes gathered after 11 o'clock last night they were clubbed by police and scattered.

Rioting between negroes and whites continued with unabated fury during the greater part of today. The disorders extended from the South Side "black belt" into the Loop, Chicago's business district, where two negroes were killed, while many others were beaten, kicked, and otherwise maltreated. The total killed since the race riots started on Sunday night is twenty-eight, while the injured number at least 500.

One unidentified negro about 28 years old, riding a bicycle, was waylaid by a mob of whites in Lyttle Street shortly after 9 o'clock tonight, stabbed and then was shot sixteen times. When the unfortunate man fell from his bicycle apparently dead, some of the rioters poured gasoline over his body, which was then set afire. Policemen were rushed to the scene, extinguished the flames and then took the charred body to the County Morgue. No arrests were made.

The "black belt" was threatened with starvation when it was learned that many firms were refusing to send delivery wagons into the district, and retailers could get no meat or groceries.

Bands of negroes were to be seen at the railroad depots, preparing to flee the city. Every train that left Chicago yesterday carried many of them, men, women, and children, some of them carrying little bundles of household articles.

The clergymen declare that practically all the clashes have been between white and negro workmen.[21]

This newspaper account reveals the scope and the level of violence which characterized the Chicago riot. It was the nation's worst race war to date, and conclusively demonstrated the readiness of the blacks to fight back. The Chicago episode was the most "fully developed" riot of the 1919 experience. It was the one in which street violence was allowed to go on the longest before outside troops were called in; and it was the one episode of interracial violence which confirmed the suspicion that such violence had deep roots in the social and economic structure of society.

A contemporary review of American press opinion concering the racial violence of the period appeared in the *Literary Digest,* and it is worth quoting here in full not only for what it reveals about the past but also for what it tells us about our own era:

Must Americans admit that they share with the Germans the cruel and bloodthirsty qualities that go with the name of "Hun"? Yes, declares the Rochester *Times-Union,* "as city after city adds to our shame," Omaha following Washington and Chicago and Boston and Knoxville, as race rioting and lynching are reported from county districts in Georgia and Arkansas, "we must realize and admit that the unthinkable, the unendurable, has actually come to pass." The Rochester editor sees us living in "an atavistic period, a throwback to the day when it was all part of the day's work to kill an offending neighbor."

"Are Americans becoming a lawless people?" asks the Philadelphia *Inquirer.* In Omaha the city was placed under martial law after a mob had lynched an offending negro, had nearly killed the mayor, and had burnt a splendid new court house with most of its records and had caused a general paralysis of business. "Think of all this happening within 24 hours," says an Iowa editor, "not in the Balkans, not in Turkey, not in Russia, but in the heart of the continent over which waves the Stars and Stripes, representing the free democracy of America." Nor is this mob rule confined to large cities which are bound to have "a disorderly element of considerable number if small proportion," as the Cleveland *News* remarks, for the tiny hamlet of Elaine in the sparsely inhabited State of Arkansas "has produced a brief reign of anarchy as serious as those disgracing some of the nation's principal cities." Evidently, the Ohio daily concludes, "there is no special danger in numbers, no particular safety in littleness." All these riots, we are told, are proving that in this country the inclination is "stronger now than ever to resort to methods outside the law." The El Paso *Times* is but one of many papers which can see no solution to the problem: "multiplied denunciations of mob violence by every agency of respectability and decency in America have resulted only in multiplied lynchings and riots." *The Times* sees things "getting worse instead of better," despite all that churches, schools and newspapers can do. The negro, we are told, is here to stay, and in increasing numbers; "every time he is made the victim of mob violence our civilization is by so much weakened; and yet we keep on lynching him." In these "orgies of lawlessness" which have disgraced six of our great cities, the Detroit *Free Press* sees the breakdown of society "under high tension following the war period." The Pittsburgh *Sun* thinks we have a "case of nerves" caused by the war, the disorder in Europe, and the delay in concluding the peace. It may be a "passing phase" but it is none the less a "danger to the future of the Republic and free institutions." Why, the St. Louis *Star* asks, is this mob spirit so manifest? Some answer, it says, "must be found before the mob becomes a greater menace to America than German militarism was to Europe."

So we find editors and representatives of both white and colored races strongly supporting the resolution of Senator Curtis (R., Kans.) calling for an investigation of, and remedies for, the race riots and lynchings which have been taking place throughout our land. A brief prepared for the use of Senatorial investigators by the National Association for the Advancement of Colored People reminds us that since the beginning of the year there have been 39 racial clashes in this country, while in the same period there have been more than 50 lynchings, all but four of the victims being negroes, of whom ten were burned at the stake. In 1918, 63 negroes and four white men were lynched and no one was ever convicted for taking part in these performances. In the years 1889–1918, 2,472 colored men and 50 colored women, 690 white men and 11 white women were lynched. In the Washington riots of last July six persons were killed and hundreds hurt. In the Chicago riots a few days later 36 persons met their death. The more recent Omaha riot caused three deaths. Less sensational race riots are held responsible for a score of killings.

No editor dares predict that a new race riot will not break out any day in any community, large or small, in North, South, East, or West. Editors who are awake to the situation generally make two demands, first, that means be employed to assert the supremacy of law over "jungle rule," and second, that the fundamental causes of the trouble be sought and a permanent remedy found. "No party of lynchers has ever been brought to justice. That might be tried," suggests the New York *Globe*. "Mob law and especially mob leadership is greatly in need of a lesson to be remembered in this country," asserts the Topeka *Capital*. The Duluth *Herald*, which regrets to see mob rule growing more menacing daily, declares that:

"There will be mobs and mob outbreaks until some day there is a legal wholesale hanging of men who have surrendered their will to the mob spirit and let it make beasts of them. And unless America wants to see every petty grievance handled by Judge Lynch, it will start that hanging bee very soon."

The police and civic authorities, as the Seattle *Post Intelligencer* notes, "are always reluctant to resort to drastic methods to quell mobs. There is always the hope that moral suasion and such comparatively harmless force as is wielded by the policemen's baton will serve a dispersing purpose. The police shoot high." The Pacific coast paper is, however, inclined to think that "the natural reaction to the Omaha outrage will be a tendency to shoot first and inquire afterwards, and one or two instances of that kind will dampen mob enthusiasm," and the editor of the *News-Herald* of Franklin, Pa., speaks for many of his brothers of the press when he says:

"The suitable answer to a mob, at the earliest possible moment when its activities become threatening to the public peace, and the only suitable answer is *bullets*; from rifles and machine guns if these are available, from police revolvers, in default of anything more effective. And, in cases like this, with the background of national outbreaks, the fire must be effective, to kill and not to frighten, and sustained as long as necessary.

"In the present condition of affairs, calling for troops is only a confession of cowardice and an admission of the weakness and inefficiency of civil government. The lawless element of the American people needs to learn that civil government is not a weak, helpless thing to be defied at will. Mobs need to learn that the police will fight; that the command of a sheriff or a mayor is backed by a power that must be feared. A hundred rioters piled dead in front of the Omaha courthouse would have been an object lesson of the majesty of the law and the wickedness and danger of resistance to law, the most valuable that could have been given.

"Something of that sort must come before this epidemic of lawlessness will be checked. In some city, the lawbreakers must meet real courage and determination, city officials who know what duty is and will do their duty and policemen who will obey the law and their oaths of service and fight. . . .

"Would to God that the next time a mob rises in any American city they might meet courage and determination that would make the streets run red with lawless blood."

. . . editors generally look upon the mob menace as a race problem. A writer in *The New York Times* declares that all observers agree that "out of the war has come a new negro problem." The negro has fought side by side with the white man and has been recognized as his equal by the French; he has become accustomed to arms and acquired a new self-respect. At the same time the war has brought new industrial contacts between white and colored workers. The writer in *The Times* estimates that "during the war period 500,000 negro workers migrated from the South to the North. In whatever Northern city they have selected in numbers there is the menace of a racial clash. "At the same time, according to this authority, there is a gradual change in the character of negro leadership. The conservative leaders of the Booker Washington type are dying out and leaders of a more militant type gain more headway every week. There are two classes of these new leaders, we are told:

"One consists of radicals and revolutionaries. They are spreading Bolshevist propaganda. It is reported that they are winning many recruits among the colored race. When the ignorance that exists among negroes in many sections of the country is taken into consideration the danger of inflaming them by revolutionary doctrine may be apprehended. It is held that there is no element in this country so susceptible to organized propaganda of this kind as the less informed class of negroes.

"The other class of militant leaders confine their agitation to a fight against all forms of color discrimination. They are for a program of uncompromising protest, 'to fight and to continue to fight for citizenship rights and full democratic privileges.'

"W. E. B. Du Bois, a foremost leader in this class of militants, says in the leading editorial in the current issue of his magazine, *The Crisis:*

" 'We have cast off on the voyage, which will lead to freedom or death. For three centuries we have suffered and cowered. No race ever gave passive submission to evil longer, more piteous trial. Today we raise the terrible weapon of self-defense. When the murderer comes, he shall no longer strike us in the back. When the armed lynchers gather, we too must gather armed. When the mob moves, we propose to meet it with bricks and clubs and guns.' "

William Monroe Trotter, Secretary of the National Equal Rights League, told the Senate Foreign Relations Committee a few weeks ago: "We are a peace-loving people, but the oppression to which negroes in America are subjected is such that unless national and state governments provide guarantees against its continuance, there can be no assurance of peace, secure from violence and insurrection." "The black man has given notice," said a New York negro on the same occasion, "that what he has suffered in the past will not be endured in the future. He means business now. There can be no compromise."

In an article in *Reconstruction*, Mr. Charles Edward Russell carefully discusses this change of attitude on the part of the negroes, which he believes must be understood as having a very definite bearing on past and future riots. To quote Mr. Russell:

"The negro did not run in Chicago nor in Washington and in my judgment he is not going to run anywhere. And the reason is that he has found himself. He knows now that he is a man. That makes the difference."[22]

There was a sharp decline of reported racial violence during the decades of the thirties. Only one major riot was recorded for the decade, the Harlem riot of 1935. But World War II brought to the surface the seething tensions which existed between the blacks and the whites. The Detroit and Harlem riots were the most violent of the era.

The Detroit race riot in 1943 was in background, in precipitating incident, and in chronology of violence much like the 1919 Chicago riot.[23]

In the background of contributing causes of the Detroit tragedy were the familiar factors still cited in the 1960's. Detroit had an abominable housing situation. Thousands of new residents had come to the city to work in the war industries, and housing was desperately short. Public facilities, including transportation and recreation, were congested. Juvenile delinquency among whites and blacks was rampant. But its basic cause was the enduring fact of American life: prejudice and misunderstanding between the two races.

The event which triggered the riot was a fist fight between a black man and a white man on a crowded bridge leading from the Belle Isle public amusement park to the city proper. Again, it was a hot Sunday night in July. A rumor had quickly spread among other blacks on the island that whites had killed a black mother and her baby and had thrown both of them in the water. The rumor was false. Nevertheless, the rumor reached Hastings Street in "Paradise Valley," the old black slum section of Detroit. Bands of blacks broke into pawnshops, stole some guns, looted white-owned stores, and stoned automobiles driven by whites. A doctor answering a late call was beaten to death. Police who rushed to the area were fired on and they fired back. Of the thirty-one known dead in the riot, fifteen were blacks shot by the city police. White gangs, barred from the black area by police guns and tear gas, took over Woodward Avenue, Detroit's main thoroughfare, where they hauled isolated blacks from autos and streetcars, beat them up, and set fire to their cars.

Captions from *Life* magazine's coverage of the riot reveal the ferocity of the violence.

Well-dressed Negro has been dragged off streetcar on Woodward Avenue and is being attacked by three white men. A fourth man looks on, smiling. After being knocked down, kicked and bloodied, Negroes were told to beat it before the cops came.

Fleeing Negro, who looks as though he is already hurt, is chased by mobsters armed with lead pipe (center) and beer bottle (right). Rioters also used stones, bricks, clubs, metal belt buckles and chunks of loose iron. Note the bandage on arm of man with lead pipe; reporters saw many members of the mob wearing fresh bandages and heard one boasting: "I killed one of 'em at 2:30 this morning."

Struggling Negro is hauled from a streetcar near downtown Detroit by four white men, while the helpless motorman looks on. In some cases mobs invaded cars and smashed Negroes' heads against floors in view of women passengers. Carmen who tried to interfere were savagely beaten.

Rioter slaps a Negro who is being held by two policemen, while a large gang of white hoodlums surges in from behind. Throughout the riot the Detroit police were tougher on Negroes than whites. They used tear gas and (sometimes) night sticks on white mobs, tommy guns and pistols on Negroes. They killed 15 Negroes, most of whom were said to be "looting," and no whites, although white gangs overturned police cars and beat up policemen in rescuing rioters who had been arrested. Note woman at left in this picture; many women were seen among the rioters.

Looted store in Negro section is inspected by distraught owner. Note single egg on shelf at the left. So many stores like this were smashed that thousands of Negro families could not get food for days after the riot. A Riot Information Bureau was established to help them.[24]

By the time the Detroit riot ended thirty-four persons had died; it was the bloodiest riot in the United States since the red summer of 1919.

The fuse to the Harlem riot was set off when a white policeman arrested a black woman for disorderly conduct.[25] A black soldier on leave who tried to stop him was shot in the shoulder after beating the officer over the head. Rumors of all kinds, none of them close to the facts, spread throughout Harlem. Crowds began gathering, seething with excitement and resentment. The black soldier became their symbol of the right to fight back. Amid the near hysteria, the crowd believed the rumor that he had been shot down and killed in cold blood in front of his aged mother. A heaved brick broke the tension, and bands of men, women, and children swarmed through Harlem, destroying and looting along the way. When it was over the next morning, five blacks were dead and about fifty policemen and over five hundred Harlem citizens were injured.[26]

These two riots were only two of the more spectacular episodes of the resurgence of racial violence during World War II. There were riots in other cities, both in the North and in the South. Nor were the riots the only kind of violence occurring during the war. There were clashes involving black military personnel which in at least a few cases came close to ending in old-fashioned lynchings.

But from the Detroit and Harlem riots of 1943 until the comparatively small-scale but large-impact race riots that occurred during 1964 in Harlem, Rochester, and a number of New Jersey cities, there were no major riots until the explosion in Watts, Los Angeles, in August, 1965. During the years of the black revolution, which really began in 1949, there was a widely held assumption that the vigorous thrust for equality had begun to close the economic gap between blacks and whites. Actually, however, the economic differences between blacks and whites not only failed to decrease but actually increased. Between 1949 and 1964 the relative participation of blacks in the total economic life of the nation declined significantly.

The background cause of the Watts riot was the demoralization of the black population of Los Angeles for many of the same reasons that such demoralization prevailed earlier in riot-torn Northern cities. Housing and employment fell desperately short of the needs of the black people. While the immediate cause of the riot was the arrest of a young black man charged with reckless driving, and the subsequent incidents which accompanied that arrest, the underlying cause was, again, the sense of injustice and frustration on the part of the black community. Killing, looting, and burning marked this episode to a degree almost unmatched by previous episodes of racial violence. "Burn, Whitey, Burn" and "Get Whitey" were introduced as slogans which were later heard over and over in the even more violent clashes of the late 1960's. By the time the police and the California National Guard restored peace, the toll had reached 34 dead, 1,032 injured, and 3,952 arrested. Property damage reached forty million dollars.[27]

The twenty-four riots in twenty-three cities which raised havoc in the nation in the summer of 1967 have been described and analyzed in remarkable depth and with persuasive insight in the seven hundred pages of the United States Riot Commission's *Report*. The violence committed by the blacks in the 1960's was racial only in the sense that it involved the attempt by one racial group to achieve "fuller participation in the social order and the material benefits enjoyed by the majority of American citizens" who belonged to another racial group, the white race.[28]

Much of the racism felt and practiced by white Americans springs from the threat such Americans *perceive* in sharing a piece of the American pie, which contains the ingredients of economic and political power. Under the threat of violence and in response to some actual violence, political power has become increasingly within the reach of black Americans and to no small degree has even been achieved. It is in the area of economic opportunity that the legislative process has so far failed in at least implementation if not in principle. It may take further violence to gain that objective, since social violence is desperation born of frustration which the regular processes of government create when they fail to fulfill the needs and aspirations of a social group.

NOTES

1. See Allen D. Grimshaw, "A Study in Social Violence: Urban Race Riots in the United States," unpublished Ph.D. dissertation (University of Pennsylvania, 1959). A more accessible although greatly condensed version of this impressive study appears under the title "Lawlessness and Violence in America and Their Special Manifestations in Changing Negro-White Relationships," *Journal of Negro History*, Vol. XLIV (1959), pp. 52–72.
2. The classical work on this subject is Herbert Aptheker's *American Negro Slave Revolts* (New York, 1943). While considerable attention has been given to this subject since the recent explosion of black historical literature, Professor Aptheker's pioneering work remains definitive, notwithstanding its Marxist orientation. A great deal of insight can be gained from an article by Raymond and Alex Bauer, "Day to Day Resistance to Slavery," *Journal of Negro History*, Vol. XXVII (1942), pp. 388–419.
3. John Hope Franklin, *From Slavery to Freedom* (New York, 1967), p. 213. This work continues to be the most scholarly if not the most readable general study of black history.
4. A vivid and well-documented account of the Draft Riots is the recently published study by James McCague, *The Second Rebellion: The Study of the New York City Draft Riots of*

1863 (New York, 1968). For younger readers Irving Wer-
stein's *July, 1863* (New York, 1957) offers a colorful and
reliable presentation. A brief but lively piece is Lawrence
Lader's "New York's Bloodiest Week," *American Heritage*,
Vol. X (1959), pp. 44–49, 95–98. Older but still important
sources include Mary L. Booth, *History of the City of New
York* (New York, 1880), pp. 818–833; Joel T. Headley,
The Great Riots of New York, 1712 to 1873 (New York,
1873), pp. 136–288; John B. McMaster, *A History of the
People of the United States During Lincoln's Administration*
(New York, 1927), pp. 407–415; and Carl Sandburg,
Abraham Lincoln: The War Years (New York, 1926), Vol.
II, pp. 360–377.

5. *The New York Times*, July 14, 1863.

6. *Ibid.*

7. *Ibid.*

8. The subject of Southern violence is crucial to any discussion
of violence in America. A significant but greatly overlooked
study is John Hope Franklin's *The Militant South* (Cambridge, Massachusetts, 1956). Fully documented and well
written, this book stands as the best available work on the
subject. Professor Sheldon Hackney surveys the literature
in the field in a recent monograph, "Southern Violence,"
American Historical Review, Vol. LXXIV (1969), pp. 906–
925, but surprisingly overlooks Franklin's work, perhaps
because Franklin does not offer any "theory" of his own.
However, the vast amount of historical material makes its
own case. Professor Hackney, after rejecting particularly
the theses of Wilbur J. Cash and John Dollard, whose studies
have received so much more recognition than Franklin's,
concludes that a "search for a valid explanation of southern
violence is needed" (p. 913). Both in this chapter and in
the chapters dealing with the violence of the abolitionist
movement and of the frontier, our own accounts are drawn
from the following books and monographs: H. C. Brearley,
"Pattern of Violence," in W. T. Couch, ed., *Culture in the
South* (Chapel Hill, 1935); Wilbur J. Cash, *The Mind of the
South* (New York, 1940; Vintage edition, 1960); John
Dollard, *Caste and Class in a Southern Town* (Garden City,
New York, 1949); Burr J. Ramage, "Homicide in the

Southern States," *Sewanee Review,* Vol. IV (1895–1896), pp. 221–230; H. V. Redfield, *Homicide: North and South* (Philadelphia, 1880); C. C. Rister, "Mob Violence in the Old South," *Mississippi Valley Historical Review,* Vol. XXIX (1942); pp. 351–370; Frank Tannenbaum, *Darker Phases of the South* (New York, 1924); and C. Vann Woodward, *Origins of the New South, 1877–1913* (New York, 1951).

9. *Cf.* Irvin G. Wyllie, "Race and Conflict on Missouri's Cotton Frontier," *Journal of Southern History,* Vol. XX (1954), pp. 183–196. Here it is argued that violence was directed against the blacks who were beginning to play an important role in the emerging cotton economy in Missouri. In short, "the record of race violence . . . suggests that behind the moral pretense was always the fact of economic interest" (p. 187).

10. See Ray S. Baker, *Following the Color Line* (New York, 1908); Ray A. Billington, *The Protestant Crusade* (New York, 1952); John M. Mecklin, *The Ku Klux Klan: A Study of the American Mind* (New York, 1963); and Gustavus Myers, *History of Bigotry in the United States* (New York, 1960).

11. Quoted in Brearley, *op. cit.,* pp. 680–681. During the American Revolution, Colonel Charles Lynch of Bedford County, Virginia, was the head of a *de facto* court which tried Tories and sentenced many of them to be whipped. Thereafter this rude punishment was held to be an example of "lynch law." While lynching originally meant a whipping, it was only in the late nineteenth and early twentieth centuries that to lynch a man came to mean to take his life. See James E. Cutler, *Lynch-Law: An Investigation into the History of Lynching in the United States* (New York, 1905). Although an older study, it is still important and useful.

12. *1957 Negro Year Book* (Tuskegee, 1957), pp. 232–257.

13. See James L. Crouthamel, "Springfield Race Riot of 1908," *Journal of Negro History,* Vol. XLV (1960), pp. 164–173.

14. "The Waco Horror," supplement to *The Crisis* (July, 1916), p. 4.

15. Quoted in *ibid.,* pp. 5–6.

16. *Ibid.,* p. 8.

17. See Arthur I. Waskow, *From Race Riot to Sit-in, 1919 and*

the 1960s (New York, 1966; Anchor edition, 1967), pp. 110–120. This is the most important work on the major race riots of 1919. The author's theory of conflict and his alternative of "creative disorder" have significant meaning today.

18. See Franklin, *From Slavery to Freedom, op. cit.*, p. 481; and Waskow, *op. cit.*, pp. 21–37.

19. *The New York Times*, June 13, 1921, p. 1.

20. The best documented study of the riot is *The Negro in Chicago: A Study of Race Relations and a Race Riot*, Chicago Commission on Race Relations (Chicago, 1922). Again, for the best retrospective analysis, see Waskow, *op. cit.*, Chapters 4, 5. A good interpretive discussion appears in Grimshaw, *op. cit.*

21. *The New York Times*, July 29, 1919.

22. *Literary Digest*, October 18, 1919, pp. 9–11.

23. For a penetrating and perceptive discussion of the background of this episode, see Earl Brown, "The Truth About the Detroit Race Riot," *Harper's Magazine*, Vol. CLXXXVII (1943), pp. 488–498. A good book-length treatment is George W. Beatly's *The Background and Causes of the 1943 Detroit Race Riot* (Princeton, New Jersey, 1954).

24. "Race War in Detroit," *Life*, Vol. XV (July 5, 1943), pp. 93–100.

25. While Mayor La Guardia himself dismissed the riot as an attempt by hoodlums intent upon "stealing from their own group and injuring their own people," a good deal more than that was involved. For the larger economic, political, and racial issues which were behind the eruption, see Walter White, "Behind the Harlem Riot," *The New Republic*, Vol. CIX (1943), pp. 220–222; and Harold Orlansky, *The Harlem Riot: A Study in Mass Frustration* (New York, 1943).

26. See "Harlem's Wild Rampage," *Life*, Vol. XV (August 16, 1943), pp. 32–33.

27. See Franklin, *From Slavery to Freedom, op. cit.*, p. 463.

28. *Report of the National Advisory Commission on Civil Disorders* (Bantam edition, New York, 1968), p. 7.

3

THE ABOLITIONIST CRUSADE

*". . . these audacious sons
of riots and disorder."*

Slavery of the black race was the subject of the conflict
between those who aimed to abolish the hated system and
those who wanted to preserve it. But the violence which
marked that conflict from the early 1800's through the
Civil War was largely between white Americans, and
almost rarely between blacks and whites. The issues were
essentially economic and political, not racial. The antiabolitionists were mostly concerned with the impact freedom for the slaves would have on the labor market and
with the potential political power of the blacks once citizenship was accorded them. The abolitionists themselves were
not much concerned about race in terms of social equality.
Political freedom was the goal of the movement and not
even political equality was given much emphasis in its
program.[1]

Mob violence against the abolitionists was part of the
American scene throughout this period. Opposition to the
American Anti-Slavery Society had been building up since

it was organized in December, 1833, and one of the longest riots on record against its supporters took place in New York City the next year. The mob first met at Chatham Street Chapel, where antislavery meetings were usually conducted. After passing resolutions approving the colonization society which proposed to deport blacks to Africa, the mob then fanned out through the city, attacking the blacks themselves. They also struck out against the white abolitionists. The house of Lewis Tappan, one of the leading abolitionists in the city, was plundered. The churches of several white ministers associated with the abolitionist movement were gutted of all furniture, benches, and pulpits. Three black churches were damaged. Order was not restored until the governor sent troops into the city.

At the end of the riot, the local press observed that

The fury of demons seems to have entered into the breasts of our misguided populace. Like those ferocious animals which, having once tasted blood, are seized with an insatiable thirst for gore, they have had an appetite awakened for outrage, which nothing but the most extensive and indiscriminate destruction seems capable of appeasing. The cabin of the poor negro, and the temples dedicated to the service of the living God, are alike the objects of their blind fury. The rights of private and public property, the obligations of law, the authority of its ministers, and even the power of the military, are all equally spurned by these audacious sons of riots and disorder.[2]

Antislavery lecturers were mobbed wherever they went. Typical of the kind of brutal violence these men were subjected to its described here by Theodore Weld of Ohio, who organized and directed the activities of the abolitionist societies in the Northwest:

> At the second lecture the mob gathered and threw stones and eggs through the window . . . The next day the mob were so loud in threats that the trustees of the church did not feel at liberty to grant the use of the vestry. The next night I lectured in a store room in the center of the village. Stones and clubs flew merrily against the shutters. At the close as I came out, curses were showered in profusion. Lamp black, nails, pockets full of stones and eggs had been provided for the occasion, and many had disguised their persons, smeared their faces, etc., to avoid recognition. Next evening same state of things, with increase of violent demonstrations . . . .[3]

Distaste and hostility toward William Lloyd Garrison, the most noted abolitionist leader, had reached its height in 1835. On October 21 of the same year, one of the most famous and violent mob scenes faced by the abolitionists took place in Boston. Garrison's uncompromising posture and such provoking episodes as his public burning of copies of the Constitution coupled with his description of it as "a covenant with death and an agreement with hell," since it guaranteed slavery, made him as hated as his cause.[4]

Together with George Thompson, a visiting English abolitionist, Garrison was to address a scheduled meeting of the Boston Female Anti-Slavery Society. This group offended not only antiabolitionists but also some masculine sensibilities. A handbill had been distributed throughout the city calling for the tarring and feathering of Thompson. A hundred-dollar reward was offered to "the individual who shall first lay violent hands on Thompson, so that he may be brought to the tar-kettle before dark."

Both the handbill and the reward were sponsored by "many of our first citizens," according to the local press. The merchant aristocracy, threatened by the loss of Southern trade if the abolitionists were not suppressed, joined and even led the mobs as they had done during the American Revolutionary period when Great Britain threatened their economic as well as their political authority.

By the time Garrison arrived at the lecture hall, about twenty-five women were seated, but a hundred more were blocked by intruders from going up the stairs into the hall. Although the woman had asked for police protection from the mayor, none was given.

The mayor himself spoke to the crowd, told them that Thompson was not in the city, and pleaded with them to break up and disperse. No one moved.

The mob cried out for Garrison. "We must have Garrison! Out with him!" Both the mayor and Garrison's friends convinced him to escape through the back of the building and avoid the crowd. He retreated across the hall to the Anti-Slavery office, which happened to be in the same building. The crowd followed him after sighting him leaping down from a back window onto a shed. He and his aides "entered a carpenter's shop, through which we attempted to get into Wilson's Lane, but found our retreat cut off by the mob." Although the carpenters tried to hide him, and one of the sheriffs in the meanwhile told the crowd that he had searched the building and that Garrison had escaped, one of the rioters managed to break into the carpenter's shop.

On seeing me, three or four of the rioters, uttering a yell, furiously dragged me to the window, with the intention of hurling me from that height to the ground; but one of them relented and said—"Don't let us kill him outright." So they drew me back, and coiled a rope about my body—probably to drag me through the streets. I bowed to the mob, and requesting them to wait patiently until I could descend, went down upon a ladder that was raised for that purpose. I fortunately extricated myself from the rope, and was seized by two or three powerful men, to whose firmness, policy, and muscular energy I am probably indebted for my preservation.[5]

An aide, Charles Burleigh, described the scene:

Going to the Post-office, I saw the crowd pouring out from Wilson's Lane into State Street with a deal of clamor and shouting, and heard the exulting cry, "They've got him— They've got him." And so, sure enough, they had. The tide set toward the south door of the City Hall, and in a few minutes I saw Garrison between two men who held him and led him along, while the throng pressed on every side, as if eager to devour him alive.[6]

After a number of close calls in which he very nearly lost his life to the rioters, Garrison was put in jail officially for disturbing the peace but actually for his own protection.[7]

An abolitionist figure who ultimately did not escape the clutches of the mob and who suffered violence resulting in death was Elijah P. Lovejoy, a Presbyterian minister who immediately after his ordination settled in the slaveholding city of St. Louis to serve as an agent of the American Home Missionary Society and as editor of the St. Louis *Observer* in 1833.[8] For the next three years he criticized slavery and advocated civil rights principles.

Under the circumstances, strong community hostility was building up against him. The crisis came in 1836.

A black boatman had accidentally killed a white man while resisting arrest. Without a trial, a mob dragged him from a jail in St. Louis, chained him to a tree, and burned him alive. Lovejoy reported the incident under the heading "Awful Murder and Savage Barbarity." He not only attacked the lynching, but he also turned his editorial wrath on a judge who appeared to support such mob justice.

When the judge had made his charge to the grand jury, he had instructed it to return no indictments if it should find that the burning of the black man was

> . . . not the act of numerable and ascertainable malefactors; but of congregated thousands, seized upon and impelled by that mysterious, metaphysical, and almost electric frenzy, which, in all ages and nations, has hurried on the infuriated multitude to deeds of death and destruction . . . If such had been the situation in that lynching, then the matter transcends your jurisdiction—it is beyond the reach of human law.[9]

Aroused by Lovejoy's editorial policy, an angry mob surrounded the *Observer*'s office at midnight on the day after the editorial appeared. While most of the people watched, about twenty men broke into the office and wrecked it. After this Lovejoy decided to move on to Alton, Illinois, where he felt he and his family would be less subjected to the violence of mobs. He had been assured by representative citizens of the city that he and his newspaper would be welcomed there.

But it was not very long before the antislavery views of his publication brought the wrath of the predominantly

proslavery forces in Alton. The Alton *Observer* had become
one of the leading liberal organs in the country. Over a
period of time a number of his presses were wrecked, and
some were dumped into the Mississippi before they could
be removed from the boats on which they were transported
to Alton. In short, Lovejoy and his cause were no less
victims of violence in the "free state" of Illinois than
they were in Missouri.

The last occasion of violence struck down both the man
and the vehicle he was using to achieve his goal of abolitionism, his press.

On Sunday, November 5, news arrived from St. Louis
that the *Missouri Fulton*, carrying a new press to replace
the one destroyed a few months earlier, would dock
at Alton on Tuesday morning at three o'clock. Lovejoy and
a group of his supporters armed themselves and stood
guard until it could be removed to the offices later in the
day. An expected attack from a local mob did not ma-
terialize and the press was safely carried to a local warehouse. Assuming that there would be no further threat
to the security of the press, at least not before morning,
all the militiamen who volunteered to help guard the
building went home, and Lovejoy and his friend, Edward
Beecher, remained alone inside the warehouse.[10]

Confident now in the press's safety, the two men left
the building. Beecher himself went out of town and Lovejoy
returned to his home. As the day passed, rumors spread
through the city that the antiabolitionists were still out to
destroy the press. By evening volunteers gathered again
at the warehouse to protect the press. Lovejoy and a few

local abolitionists also returned to the warehouse to protect it.

About ten o'clock a mob, already armed, came and formed
a line at the end of the store in Water Street, and hailed those
within. Mr. Gilman opened the door of the third story, and
asked what they wanted. They demanded the press. He, of
course, refused to give it up; and earnestly entreated them to
use no violence. . . . They then went to the other end of the
store and commenced an attack. They demolished two or
three windows with stones and fired two or three guns. As
those within threw back the stones, one without was distinctly
recognized and seen taking aim at one within: for it was a
moonlight evening, and persons could be distinctly seen and
recognized.

A few guns were then fired by individuals from within, by
which Lyman Bishop, one of the mob, was killed. . . . After
this the mob retired for a few moments, and then returned with
ladders which they lashed together to make them the proper
length, and prepared to set fire to the roof.

About this time the mayor, having been informed of the
riot, came on to the ground; but having few to sustain him,
was unable to compel the rioters to desist by force. They
requested him to go into the store, and state to its defenders
that they were determined to have the press; and would not
desist until they had accomplished their object; and agreed
to suspend operations until his return. Attended by a justice
of the peace, he entered and delivered the message of the
mob. . . .

However, they did not give it up. Mr. Gilman requested
the mayor to call on certain citizens, to see if they could not
prevent the destruction of the building. He said he could not:
he had used his official authority in vain. He then asked him
whether he should continue to defend the property by arms.
This the mayor, as he had previously done, authorized him to

do. The mayor and the justice were then informed that the press would not be given up, and the decision was by them communicated to the mob. They then proceeded to fire the roof, taking care to keep on the side of the store where they were secure from the fire of those within.

It now became evident to the defenders that their means of defense, so long as they remained within, was cut off; and nothing remained but to attack the assailants without. It was a hazardous step; but they determined to take it. A select number, of whom Mr. Lovejoy was one, undertook the work. They went out at the end, turned the corner, and saw one of the incendiaries on the ladder, and a number standing at the foot. They fired and it is supposed wounded, but did not kill him; and then, after continuing their fire some minutes and dispersing the mob, returned to load their guns. When they went out again no one was near the ladder, the assailants having so secreted themselves as to be able to fire, unseen, on the defenders of the press as they came out. No assailants being in sight Mr. Lovejoy stood, and was looking round. Yet, though he saw no assailant, the eye of his murderer was on him. The object of hatred, deep, malignant, and long continued, was fully before him—and the bloody tragedy was consummated. Five balls were lodged in his body, and he soon breathed his last. Yet after his mortal wound he had strength remaining to return to the building and ascend one flight of stairs before he fell and expired. They then attempted to capitulate, but were refused with curses by the mob, who threatened to burn the store and shoot them as they came out. Mr. Roff now determined at all hazards to go out and make some terms, but he was wounded as soon as he set foot over the threshold.

The defenders then held a consultation. They were shut up within the building, unable to resist the ferocious mode of attack now adopted, and seemed devoted to destruction. At length Mr. West came to the door, informed them that the building was actually on fire, and urged them to escape by passing down the riverbank, saying that he would stand between them and the assailants so that if they fired they must fire on him. This was done. All but two or three marched out and ran down Water Street. Two, who were wounded, were left in the building, and one, who was not, remained to take care of the body of their murdered brother. The mob then entered, destroyed the press, and retired. . . .

Before these tragic scenes were ended, the streets were crowded with spectators. . . .

The feelings exhibited by the mob were in keeping with the deed on which they were intent. Oaths, curses, blasphemy, and malignant yells broke upon the silence of the night as they prosecuted their work of death. But even passions so malignant were not enough to give them the hardihood and recklessness needed for their work. To drench conscience, blind reason, and arouse passion to its highest fury the intoxicating cup was needed to fit them for the consummation of their work. The leaders in this business were adepts; they knew what means were adapted to their ends, and used them without stint or reason.[11]

The Alton riots and the murder of Lovejoy left no feelings of remorse in Alton, where the antiabolitionists continued to reign, but they did have great impact on Northern opinion in terms of arousing the abolitionist movement as no other event did until the execution of John Brown in 1859.[12]

Lovejoy's fate raised the problem of violence in the antislavery movement again, a problem faced at the outset of the movement during the first great mushrooming of antislavery societies in the 1830's.[13] Every new society's constitution contained a disclaimer that the society would never resort to force to achieve its aims. Truth was to be its only force. At first, however, it was in terms of slave insurrections that the abolitionists were thinking. Slave revolt was considered wrong in principle and impolitic as well.

As indeed was true, there were too few blacks too inade-
quately equipped to fight on even terms with their masters.
Besides, abolitionists thought they could more easily get
Northern support through a nonviolent course of action.

But there was an ambivalence in this posture. Abolitionists did hold out the prospect of insurrection as a kind of
threat with which to prod the slaveholders into making
immediate plans for emancipation. There were occasions
when abolitionists did not turn the other cheek and did
fight back when they were victims of riotous mobs. Lovejoy
and his friends did arm themselves and in their futile
attempt to protect the press on which their antislavery newspaper was printed shot and killed at least one of the
local rioters who invaded the warehouse. Again, reaction
of many abolitionists was quite ambivalent. They felt a
deep sorrow at the death of Lovejoy and they decried the
mob spirit which brought it about. Yet they regretted that
the Alton reformers allowed themselves to be provoked
into taking up arms in self-defense.

After 1845 nonviolent principles began to fall apart in
much of the abolitionist movement. "Moral power," argued
one Southerner in the movement, "must always be backed
with cold steel and the flashing blade." By the 1850's the
conversion of the movement to violent means was fairly
complete. There is something about all this which recalls
the shift from nonviolence to violence in the present-day
black struggle.[14]

Not surprisingly, in the light of our observations about
Southern violence in another section of this book, mob
violence in the South against the abolitionists reached a
greater intensity than it ever achieved in the North. Here,

the social (racial), economic, and political effects of immediate emancipation were enough to panic every class of society. Everyone shared in the stake of racial control of the black man.[15]

While antislavery propaganda in the North resulted in violent attacks on freedom of the press such as in the Lovejoy episode, the violent attacks in the South provoked by antislavery publications were far more numerous and widespread. A mob headed by a former governor, Robert Y. Hayne, invaded the Charleston, South Carolina, post office and destroyed sacks of mail holding abolition literature. Vigilance committees met incoming ships and searched them for such material. The duty of each local vigilante committee was

> . . . to detect and to bring to speedy punishment all emissaries who may be found within the borders of our county, giving circulation to the papers or pamphlets put forth by the Abolitionist Associations of the North, agitating the question of slavery, and therefore endangering the peace and tranquility of our land.[16]

Like the earlier Revolutionary patriots, they established committees of correspondence to keep in touch with similar committees throughout the South. When Southerners emigrated to the West, they carried with them this experience and put it to use during the period of frontier violence in the late nineteenth century when vigilance committees reigned.

The violence of the antiabolitionists did not succeed in destroying the movement, however many individual abolitionists they murdered and however much of their property they destroyed. Again, D. H. Lawrence's "essential white American" turned to violence when no other means served his end. It took the total "legitimate" military violence of the Civil War to resolve the *political* issues involved in the abolitionist movement. The ethnic or racial issue, as well as the economic issue, is still with us. And the impulse to resolve conflict with violence still threatens. Tradition dies hard.

NOTES

1. Two excellent documentary studies dealing with the abolitionists are Martin B. Duberman, ed., *The Antislavery Vanguard: New Essays on the Abolitionists* (Princeton, New Jersey, 1965); and Louis Ruchames, ed., *The Abolitionists: A Collection of Their Writings* (New York, 1963). Two other studies, while aimed at secondary school and college students, are useful for the general reader interested in the controversial questions dealing with the abolitionist movement: Richard Curry, ed., *Abolitionists: Reformers or Fanatics?* (New York, 1965); and Bernard A. Weisberger, ed., *Abolitionism: Disrupter of the Democratic System or Agent of Progress?* (Chicago, 1963).
2. New York *Evening Post*, July 12, 1834.
3. Theodore Weld, *American Slavery as It Is: Testimony of a Thousand Witnesses* (New York, 1893), p. 19.
4. See Louis Filler, *The Crusade Against Slavery* (New York, 1960); and Lawrence Lader, *The Bold Brahmins, New England's War Against Slavery* (New York, 1961).
5. Quoted in John Jay Chapman, *William Lloyd Garrison* (Boston, 1921), pp. 115–116.
6. Quoted in *ibid.*, p. 116.
7. The complaint and warrant may be of interest to the reader:

> *To Edward G. Prescott, Esquire, one of the Justices of the Peace within and for the County of Suffolk.*
>
> Daniel Parkman, of said Boston, Esquire, complains and gives said Justice to understand and be informed that William Lloyd Garrison, of Boston, in said county, printer, together with divers other persons to the number of thirty or more to your complainant unknown, on the twenty-first day of October, instant, at Boston, aforesaid, in the county aforesaid, did, as your complainant verily believes and has no doubt, unlawfully, riotously, and routously assemble, and then and there did disturb and break the peace of the Commonwealth, and a riot did cause and make, to the terror of the good people of the Commonwealth, and against the peace and dignity of the same.
>
> Therefore, your complainant prays that the said William Lloyd Garrison may be apprehended and dealt with as to law and justice shall appertain.
>
> Dated at Boston, this twenty-first day of October, in the year of our Lord one thousand eight hundred and thirty-five.
>
> Daniel Parkman

This item appears in Ellis Ames, "Garrison Mob," *Proceedings of the Massachusetts Historical Society*, Vol. XVIII (1881), p. 341.

8. Among the more recent full-length works on Lovejoy are Merton L. Dillon, *Elijah P. Lovejoy, Abolitionist Editor* (Urbana, Illinois, 1961); and John Gill, *Tide Without Turning: Elijah P. Lovejoy and Freedom of the Press* (Boston, 1958).

9. *Missouri Republican*, May 26, 1836.

10. Beecher was the son of Lyman Beecher, a nationally renowned orthodox minister of the period, and brother of Henry Ward and Harriet, both of whom achieved great fame in later years. His account, *Narrative of Riots in Alton: In Connection with the Death of Rev. Elijah P. Lovejoy* (Alton, 1838), which is nearly contemporary with the event, is extensively used in this study. A recent paperback edition was published by E. P. Dutton under the title, *Narrative of Riots*

at Alton (New York, 1965), and includes an excellent introduction by Robert Meredith.

11. *Ibid.*, pp. 63–66 (Dutton paperback edition).
12. See Dillon, *op. cit.*, p. 177.
13. See J. Demos, "Antislavery Movement and Problems of Violent Means," *New England Quarterly*, Vol. XXXVII (1964), pp. 501–526.
14. See Sylvan S. Tomkins, "The Psychology of Commitment: The Constructive Role of Violence and Suffering for the Individual and for His Society," in Martin B. Duberman, ed., *The Antislavery Vanguard, op. cit.*, Chapter 12, n. 1.
15. See Clement Eaton, "Mob Violence in the Old South," *Mississippi Valley Historical Review*, Vol. XXIX (1943), pp. 351–370.
16. Quoted in *ibid.*, p. 358.

4

POLITICAL AUTHORITY
AND RESISTANCE

"When the smoke cleared,
five Bostonians lay dead or dying in the street."

Violence and the threat of violence were very much a part
of the American Revolutionary movement. It was present,
as the elder Arthur Schlesinger wrote,

> . . . at every significant turning point of the events leading up
> to the War for Independence. Mobs terrified the stamp agents
> into resigning and forced a repeal of the tax. Mobs obstructed
> the execution of the Townshend Revenue Act and backed up
> the boycotts of British trade. Mobs triggered the Boston Mas-
> sacre and later the famous Tea Party . . . Later civilian mobs
> behind the lines systematically intimidated Tory opponents,
> paralyzing their efforts or driving them into exile.[1]

From the time of the first settlements mob violence and
rioting were commonplace in the American colonies. All
the major cities at one time or another suffered the
destructive consequences of mob rioting. In the countryside,

too, aggrieved farmers frequently destroyed property, closed courts, and brought government to a halt.[2]

In Boston, perhaps the best policed and most orderly city in colonial America, a mob of women, armed, it was said, with chamber pots, assaulted the troops returning from the abortive Canadian expedition of 1707; there were riots in 1710 and in 1713 in protest against grain exports at a time of shortage, and then again, for equally specific purposes, in 1721, 1725, 1729, 1741, 1745 (when Guy Fawkes Day parades led to a free-for-all in which several rioters were killed), and in 1747 (when a mob numbering thousands, protesting against impressment into the Royal Navy, put an end to all government and law enforcement for several days). So too mobs in Charleston, Newport, Philadelphia, and New York kept law enforcement officers at bay despite the passage of riot acts; in 1759 and 1760 antimilitary riots were so severe in Philadelphia that it was suggested that the commander-in-chief divert forces from the campaigns against the French and Indians to put them down. Nor, throughout the eighteenth century, was rioting only an urban phenomenon. In 1711 several hundred Palatines, enraged at the treatment they had received in their settlement on the upper Hudson, marched against the governor and the landlords, and were kept in control only by a show of force. In New Jersey repeatedly between 1745 and 1754 there were violent uprisings of farmers protesting against the collection of quitrents and the manipulation of land titles: an estimated one third of the farmers in certain counties were involved: jails were thrown open, courts were stopped, and property destroyed.

In the fifties violence among contending factions in the Connecticut-New York border area was so intense and continuous that it approached open warfare; and in the Carolina back country, where lawlessness was so widespread that society as such seemed scarcely to exist, the would-be "regulators" of the outlaws proved at times to be indistinguishable from the mobs they sought to control.[3]

All of this is in sharp contrast to the traditional picture of a dignified movement of protest stemming from lofty constitutional principles and led by men of stature like James Otis, John Adams, John Dickinson, and Thomas Jefferson.

Opposition to the Stamp Act initiated a whole series of violent activities during the pre-Revolutionary period. While the most effective resistance was probably the non-violent boycott of English importations, the violence used to force the resignation of men appointed to distribute the stamped paper played no small part in the eventual cancellation of the hated tax.

The first violence in response to this act occurred in Boston on the night of August 14, 1765. Governor Bernard described the episode to Lord Halifax:

Castle William, August 15, 1765

My Lords,

I am extremely concerned, that I am obliged to give your Lordships the Relation that is to follow; as it will reflect disgrace upon this Province, and bring the Town of Boston under great difficulties. Two or three months ago, I thought that this People would have submitted to the Stamp Act without actual Opposition. Murmurs indeed were continually heard, but they seemed to be such as would in time die away; but the publishing [of] the Virginia Resolves proved an Alarm Bell to be disaffected. From that time an infamous weekly Paper, which is printed here, has swarmed with libells of the most atrocious kind. These have been urged with so much Vehemence and so industriously repeated, that I have considered them as preludes

to Action. But I did not think, that it would have commenced
so early, or be carried to such Lengths, as it has been.

Yesterday morning at break of day was discovered hanging
upon a Tree in a Street of the Town an Effigy, with inscriptions,
shewing that it was intended to represent Mr. Oliver, the
Secretary, who has lately accepted the office of Stamp Dis-
tributor. Some of the Neighbours offered to take it down, but
they were given to know, that would not be permitted. Many
Gentlemen, especially some of the Council, treated it as a boyish
sport, that did not deserve the Notice of the Governor and
Council. But I did not think so; however, I contented myself
with the Lt. Governor, as Chief Justice, directing the Sheriff
to order his Officers to take down the Effigy; and I appointed
a Council to meet in the Afternoon to consider what should be
done, if the Sheriff's Officers were obstructed in removing the
Effigy.

Before the Council met, the Sheriff reported, that his Officers
had endeavoured to take down the Effigy; but could not do it
without imminent danger to their lives. The Council met;
I represented this Transaction to them as the beginning, in my
Opinion, of much greater Commotions. I desired their Advice,
what I should do upon this Occasion. A Majority of the
Council spoke in form against doing anything but upon very
different Principles; some said, that it was trifling Business,
which, if let alone, would subside of itself, but if taken notice
of would become a serious Affair. Others said, that it was a
serious Affair already; that it was a preconcerted Business,
in which the greatest Part of the Town was engaged; that
we had no force to oppose to it, and making an Opposition
to it, without a power to support the Opposition, would only
inflame the People; and be a means of extending the mischief
to persons not at present the Objects of it. Tho' the Council
were almost unanimous in advising, that nothing should be
done, they were averse to having such advice entered upon the
Council Book. But I insisted upon their giving me an Answer
to my Question, and that it should be entered in the Book;

when, after a long altercation, it was avoided by their advising me to order the Sheriff to assemble the Peace Officers and preserve the peace which I immediately ordered, being a matter of form rather than of real significance. It now grew dark when the Mob, which had been gathering all the Afternoon, came down to the Town House, bringing the Effigy with them, and knowing we were sitting in the Council Chamber, they gave three Huzzahs by way of defiance, and passed on. From thence they went to a new Building, lately erected by Mr. Oliver to let out for Shops, and not quite finished; this they called the Stamp Office, and pulled it down in five minutes. From thence they went to Mr. Oliver's House; and broke all the Windows next the Street; then they carried the Effigy to Fort Hill near Mr. Oliver's House, where they burnt the Effigy in a Bonfire made of the Timber they had pulled down from the building. Mr. Oliver had removed his family from his House, and remained himself with a few friends, when the Mob returned to attack the House. The Mob finding the Doors barricaded, broke down the whole fence of the Garden towards Fort Hill, and coming on beat in all the Doors and Windows of the Garden front, and entered the House, the Gentlemen there retiring. As soon as they had got Possession, they searched about for Mr. Oliver, declaring they would kill him; finding that he had left the House, a party set out to search two neighbouring Houses, in one of which Mr. Oliver was, but happily they were diverted from this pursuit by a Gentleman telling them, that Mr. Oliver was gone with the Governor to the Castle. Otherwise he would certainly have been murdered. After 11 o'clock the Mob seeming to grow quiet, the (Lt. Governor) Chief Justice and the Sheriff ventured to go to Mr. Oliver's House to endeavour to persuade them to disperse. As soon as they began to speak, a Ringleader cried out "The Governor and the Sheriff! to your arms, my boys!" Presently after a volley of Stones followed, and the two Gentlemen narrowly escaped thro' favour of the Night not without some bruises. I should have mentioned before, that I sent a written order to the Colonel of the Regiment of Militia, to beat an Alarm; he answered, that it would signify nothing, for as soon as the drum was heard, the drummer would be knocked down, and the drum broke; he added, that probably all the drummers of the Regiment were in the Mob. Nothing more being to be done, the Mob were left to disperse at their own Time, which they did about 12 o'clock.[4]

Another example of lawlessness and violence during these years leading up to the open war between the Colonies and Britain was the burning of the British revenue schooner *Gaspee*, near Providence, Rhode Island, at midnight on June 9, 1772. While the ship was looking for local smugglers who were seeking to avoid paying taxes on imports from abroad, it ran aground near Providence. During the night a band of citizens boarded it, sent the crew ashore, and put a torch to the vessel.

Of course the best-known incident was the Boston Tea Party late in the following year.[5] In 1773 the English East India Company, heavily in debt, had in its warehouses a mountain of unsold tea. If it could sell the tea, its problems would be solved. Parliament obliged the company by passing the Tea Act. It provided for the direct sale of tea by the East India Company to its agents in America, thus bypassing the American merchants engaged in the tea business and eliminating their profits as middlemen. The company was to be permitted to ship the tea to America from the mother country without first paying the regular duty for bringing it into England. Only the three-pence duty would be laid on the tea sold in the Colonies.

The American patriots knew that if the East India Company's tea was once landed, it would be sold and drunk. Americans would, in effect, be admitting that England had the right to establish the kind of monopoly it had given to the East India Company. So the radicals spread propaganda among the colonists, saying that the East India tea was not good; that it had been sweating for several years in a warehouse; that in fact tea was bad for one's health, anyway.

Opposition to the Tea Act reached its peak in Boston. There a band of men disguised as Mohawk Indians went aboard the tea ships in the harbor on the night of December 16, 1773. Samuel Adams, jumping to his feet in the crowded Old South Church, gave the prearranged signal with his cry that that meeting could do nothing more to save the country.[6] A war whoop broke out and a band of made-up Mohawks began their march to Griffin's wharf.

Although accounts differ, most witnesses agreed that the active participants numbered between thirty and sixty and were divided into three groups, each with a competent leader. While two parties clambered aboard *Dartmouth* and *Eleanor,* the brig *Beaver,* lying off the wharf, was warped alongside. The customs officers on board each vessel were forced ashore, and the squads began their work. Some men dropped into the hold to attach block and tackle to the heavy chests; others hoisted them to the deck. A third gang broke them open with axes, shoveled and poured the tea over the side, and heaved the chests after it. The tide was nearly low, and the water was only two or three feet deep. Soon the tea began to pile up, threatening to spill back into the vessels. Men pushed it aside as best they could to make room for more.[7]

The event brought to a head the conflict between the Colonies and their mother country. Britain's response was the repressive Boston Port Bill, an attempt to starve the riotous city into submission.

That most famous of all pre-Revolutionary episodes of violence, the Boston Massacre, was preceded and provoked by months of riotous acts on the part of the local population against the British soldiers who were stationed in the city. The episode remains in the no man's land of the "facts" of American history. Professor John C. Miller's secondary narrative account is perhaps one of the most reliable in view of the primary documents he used.

On the night of March 5, 1770, when a mob of citizens began to attack the sentry at the customhouse, Captain Preston concluded that the Whigs intended to loot the King's Chest in which the customs revenue was stored. Quickly gathering reinforcements, he drew his men up before the customhouse and attempted to parley with the mob. He found, however, that the townspeople were in no mood to reason: they were striking "their Clubs or Bludgeons one against another and calling out, "come on you Rascals, you bloody-backs, you Lobster-Scoundrels; fire if you dare, G-d damn you, fire and be damned, we know you dare not.'" Prescott stood between the mob and the soldiers, attempting to make his voice heard above the din, when the mob "advanced to the points of the Bayonets, struck some of them, and even the Muzzles of the Pieces, and seemed to be endeavouring to close with the Soldiers." At this moment, after one of the soldiers had been knocked down the command "fire" was heard and the soldiers emptied their guns into the mob. Preston was later accused of having ordered his men to fire; he denied the charge and it is improbable that he gave such a command. At the time of the volley, Preston was directly in the line of fire and came perilously near being struck himself.

When the smoke cleared, five Bostonians lay dead or dying

in the street. The townspeople immediately fell back; but after a few moments of hesitation they came forward again, apparently to take away the dead and wounded. The soldiers, however, believed that they were to be attacked again and they began to make ready to fire until Preston struck up their firelocks with his own hand. After the street had been cleared, there could be little doubt that the mob was preparing a second attack. The streets echoed to the beat of drums and the cry of "To Arms! To Arms! To Arms! Turn out with your guns!" Preston was told that four or five hundred people were assembling and had sworn to take the life of every British soldier that had fired upon the citizens. Rather than face this overwhelming force, Preston and his men retreated until they were joined by the 29th Regiment, which had gotten under arms. Although several officers were knocked down by missiles before they finally reached the guardhouse, no casualties were suffered and the danger of a counter massacre was averted at least for the night.[8]

Even after independence was won from Britain, two major episodes of violence were directed against the duly constituted political authority of the *American* government. The first event, Shays' Rebellion, was conducted against state sovereignty under the Articles of Confederation; and the second, the Whiskey Rebellion, was a challenge to the sovereignty of the federal government. Resistance to constituted authority as a means of redressing grievances had been successful so many times during the pre-Revolutionary period that it was easily argued that what had been done before could be done again.

After the close of the Revolutionary War most of the states were forced to levy high taxes to pay off the states' indebtedness resulting from the costs of that war. The taxes had to be paid in specie, actual coin. There was very little such hard money in the country. Farmers had the least cash of all, and they needed all they could get their hands on for necessities which they could not produce themselves.

It was in the rural areas of western Massachusetts where the economic hardship was greatest for the farmers. Almost every farmer owed money to some merchant. The Eastern merchants were as much in the loan business as in trade. They had loaned the farmers money to buy land, or to increase their acreage, or to get livestock and tools. Since sound currency had become almost extinct, these outstanding loans became burdensome to both debtor and creditor, for the merchant creditors demanded interest and principal in hard money. The merchants had enough influence with the legislatures to ensure that no law would require them to accept paper money or goods in payment of a debt.

This contest over paper money took the form of a test of strength in Massachusetts between the prosperous coastal towns and the small farmers of the interior, who found it increasingly difficult to pay their debts and taxes. Those attending angry town meetings and conventions sent instructions to their representatives in the General Court, as the Massachusetts legislature was called, to have the courts suspend judgments on debtors until more hard money was available. They were also instructed either to make personal property a legal satisfaction of a claim or to issue paper money and make it legally acceptable for payments of debts and taxes.[9]

The General Court did not pass any measures which would help the poor and the debt-ridden. There was no interest on the part of the merchants who dominated the Court in paper money already available, nor were they at all interested in issuing more of it.

In 1781 returning veterans of the just-concluded War of Independence were filled with disillusionment at the system of government that had been established in their absence. After having shed their blood, they were discouraged by the fact that they would be subject to burdensome taxes at home, and if they could not pay their creditors, to jail sentences as well.

Once it became clear that the General Court was not going to be responsive to their grievances against the new taxes and the court judgments on helpless debtors, mobs of poor farmers in various areas rioted in protest.

In the spring of 1782 Preacher Samuel Cullick Ely of the Sunderland congregation incited the distressed farmers to join together to prevent the judges from holding court and arresting more debtors. He reminded the agitated farmers that closing the courts had been a way of protecting the rebellious colonists from British recriminations. The pre-Revolutionary Colonial experience had established the precedent of taking the law into one's own hands when it was perceived to be abusive (we will see in a later chapter that the farmers in the Depression of the 1930's continued this violent tradition in recent times).

On April 12 Ely did lead the farmers into Northampton to keep the judges from sitting, but a group of veterans in the town prevented Ely and his followers from carrying out their objective. The courts sat.[10]

For the next four years groups of farmers in the backwoods country made abortive attempts to obstruct the courts' work in arresting debtors. And during this same period the General Court remained unresponsive to petitions by the farmers for relief.

By 1786 the state treasury was about empty as a result of an economic depression which prevailed in the state. In August and September of that year the situation had become so serious that armed farmers did succeed in closing down courts attempting to carry out foreclosure proceedings.[11]

On September 29, fearing indictments from the Supreme Court at Springfield, Captain Daniel Shays, a Revolutionary War captain who was "drafted" by a committee of Hampshire County farmers to lead their insurrection, led about eight hundred insurgents and demanded adjournment of the Court. Confronted by the militia, Shays made a compromise before any violence occurred, and the Court adjourned. The meeting of the legislature in November brought no redress, and Governor James Bowdoin advocated the use of force to suppress the uprising.

Now terrified, the conservative Eastern merchants closed ranks to suppress the rebellion. General Benjamin Lincoln was appointed to lead a force against the rebels on January 1. When the state government was unable to provide funds for his 4,400 troops, Lincoln raised the money in twenty-four hours among the Boston merchants, who were persuaded that they must give part of their wealth to save the remainder. Lincoln proceeded at once toward Springfield, the location of the federal arsenal, which was believed to be a certain objective of Shays. Shays was to have combined forces with Luke Day, one of the leading figures in the rebellion, second only to Shays in importance, and in command of some four hundred men. However, Day failed to meet up with Shays as planned, and as a result the state militia and federal troops routed Shays. Shays now moved secretly to Petersham, during which time letters were passing between him and Lincoln about a truce; but Lincoln and his troops, after a thirty-mile nightime trek through a snowstorm, made a surprise attack on the rebels and effectively crushed the rebellion. Less than a dozen lives were lost in the four years of the epidemic of mob movements against the courts and revenue officers, and half of these were lost during the actual "battles" in 1786.[12]

When the rebellion was effectively crushed, conservatives continued to fear for the safety of their property. In March Shays and other rebel leaders were tried and sentenced to death, but they were later pardoned. The state yielded to some of the farmers' demands by granting tax relief and allowing postponement of debt payments. But the major significance and outcome of the rebellion was that it convinced conservatives in various parts of the country that only a strong national government could keep discontented mobs from getting control of state governments. It was, then, this uprising in Massachusetts which helped to precipitate the calling of a national convention to revise the structure of the national government under the Articles of Confederation. What resulted was not a revision but a replacement in the form of a new constitution establishing a strong central government within the framework of a federal union.[13]

Thomas Jefferson not only approved the use of violence in this episode, but he even suggested that a "little rebellion" every once in a while is a good thing for a democratic government:

> God forbid we should ever be twenty years without such a rebellion . . . The tree of liberty must be refreshed from time to time, with the blood of patriots and tyrants. It is a natural manure.[14]

The Whiskey Rebellion of 1794, taking place within a few years of the adoption of the Constitution, was one of the decisive events in early American history.[15] This was the last time the authority of the federal government was challenged by violent political resistance until the firing on Fort Sumter in 1861.*

When the new government began to function in 1789, its main source of money came from the sale of public lands. But the national government needed more funds than such sales could produce. Young Alexander Hamilton, Washington's Secretary of the Treasury, urged Congress to levy a tax on distilled liquor. The tax he had in mind was an excise tax which the distiller himself would have to pay for every gallon of liquor he produced and sold.

It was doubtful that Hamilton really expected to raise much revenue from such a tax. He had another objective in mind, and that was to impress the frontiersmen with the power of the federal government. Reaching into the back country and lifting money from the pockets of independent-minded frontiersmen by taxing them for every gallon of whiskey they distilled would certainly make a point.

---

* The Civil War was of course the most violent political episode in American history, but since this was "legitimate" military violence it is outside the scope of this work.

To understand why this proposal was a provocation it is important to bear in mind frontier conditions in the 1790's. The frontiersmen were almost isolated from the settled areas along the Atlantic coast. Travelers could move back and forth only over the roughest of trails through the forests. As a result, the frontiersmen could not hope to transport the corn they grew to markets in the settled areas. Yet corn was their most important crop, and they could and did distill the corn into whiskey, which they then loaded in jugs or kegs onto the backs of mules and drove the mules eastward to market. Clearly, whiskey was the most important source of cash for many of the farmers who lived on the frontier. The excise tax hit them hard.

Not unexpectedly, the frontiersmen refused to pay the tax, and a rebellion was on. Small farmers in western Pennsylvania resorted to violence. They attacked federal revenue officers who tried to collect the tax, and frequently tarred and feathered them. It was in western Pennsylvania that the uprising against the federal government's authority to impose and collect the tax took on the proportions of an organized revolt in 1791, shortly after the law was enacted on March 3.

President George Washington fired off a proclamation on September 15, 1792, countersigned by his Secretary of State, Thomas Jefferson (apparently it was too soon for another "little rebellion"), warning disloyal westerners that they must "desist from all unlawful combinations and proceedings whatsoever, having for object or tending to obstruct the operation of the laws." In no uncertain terms the President made it clear that the excise would be enforced.[16]

Although the year 1793 was quieter than the preceding one, there were moments of violence. But this violence was again limited to burning collectors in effigy and sometimes burning down their homes. But by 1794 the farmer-distillers broadened their violence to include the law-abiding distillers. Barns were burned and so were hay and grain. The shooting up of stills came to be the trademark of roving bands of men who were violently opposed to the whiskey tax. The practice was known as "mending the still." One of the ringleaders, describing those taking part in such "mending" operations, coined the phrase "Tom the Tinker's Boys"—a tinker being an itinerant peddler who mended pots and pans. This became the popular name for violent opponents of the whiskey tax. Notices warning against compliance with the law, ominously signed "Tom the Tinker," were tacked up in all conspicuous spots.

Furthermore, the law required every still to be registered for inspection at the proper local office by the end of June. But so stiff had the resistance become that by June 20 the chief collector admitted that in Allegheny County not a single still had been registered. And Tom the Tinker's Boys were hard at work in every other county, closing the offices so that it would be impossible for the distillers to obey the law. One night the inspector in Washington County was, typically, brought out of his house and taken into the woods where his assailants shaved off his hair, tarred and feathered him, and tied him to a tree.

One of the most objectionable features of the excise tax was the provision requiring those prosecuted for violations to stand trial in federal courts which were often very far away (the one nearest the Pittsburgh district, for example,

was in Philadelphia, three hundred and fifty miles away).
Besides forcing farmers to halt all work to attend court,
the cost of the trip itself was equivalent to a heavy fine.
In June, 1794, Congress acted on Hamilton's request and
permitted state courts to exercise jurisdiction over excise
cases in those areas more than fifty miles from the nearest
federal court. Far from being received as a concession,
however, this act was looked upon as inflammatory, for
its application was specifically withheld from "distillers
who had previously to its enactment incurred a penalty."
To make matters worse, in May, 1794, the federal court
in Philadelphia had issued writs against seventy-five western Pennsylvania distillers which were returnable in that
court, but had delayed until July to serve them. When
federal marshals came west with the writs, they were
attacked by a mob shouting, "The federal sheriff is taking
men away to Philadelphia!"

The situation had grown so serious in western Pennsylvania that President Washington concluded that he must
take action. On August 4 Supreme Court Justice James
Wilson issued a statement certifying that the western
counties were in a state of insurrection. Three days later,
on August 7, Washington declared in a proclamation that
the outbreaks of violence were "acts which I am advised
amount to treason, being acts of levying war against the
United States. . . . Flagrant defiance of the law must be
met by force." Secretary of War Knox issued orders to
the governors of four states to call up and hold in readiness
thirteen thousand militia for use against the insurgents.

The army that President Washington put into the field
to quell this rebellion was larger than any he had ever

commanded in a single action during the Revolution. It was strictly a militia army, however, and there had been problems in raising it. Men who remembered their Revolutionary service balked at enrolling again. When conscription was put in effect, riots broke out in sections of Maryland and Pennsylvania. Finally a substantial army was raised and began to move into the western frontier of Pennsylvania. For all practical purposes, the insurrection was over at that point, because with the approach of this sizable army, any thought of resistance was fast melting away. By early November the army had occupied the entire area, and the insurrection was formally at an end. There was a short but violent period of occupation during which the ringleaders managed to escape the region. Two men were convicted of treason and sentenced to death, but Washington eventually stepped in and pardoned them.

Thus the whiskey tax proposed by Hamilton to provide the federal government with an excuse to demonstrate its authority also succeeded in providing a challenge to that authority, stirring up both ideological and economic grievances to the point where one small section of the nation violently opposed it. Opponents of the tax in other sections of the country were just as vociferous in their denunciation of it and just as hostile to its enforcement, but it was only in western Pennsylvania that this opposition resulted in violence, because at this time recognition of the political authority of the central government was strong enough throughout the nation as a whole to prevent such violence. Almost seventy years were to pass before political, economic, and above all, moral and social factors overcame this "consensus" and led to the Civil War, which was the ultimate challenge to central political authority in this country.

Not until our own time was the authority of the federal government again challenged through the use of violence. In 1962 the campus of the University of Mississippi was the scene of such an episode of political violence.[18] While the underlying element was racism, the violence was directed against the federal government's attempt to enforce an order of its courts.

It seems totally anachronistic that in the 1960's the old States' rights doctrine should even be argued let alone considered an issue to be resolved by armed conflict. It had been resolved empirically by the Civil War and judicially by decisions of the Supreme Court. In 1932 Chief Justice Charles Evans Hughes declared it to be "manifest" that a state governor could not invoke his powers to infringe anyone's rights under the federal constitution. In 1954 the Court unanimously ruled that segregation in public schools violated the Fourteenth Amendment, and four years later in the Little Rock decision, the Court held unanimously that the school desegregation decision of 1954 "can neither be nullified by state executive or judicial officers nor nullified indirectly by them through evasive schemes."

On May 31, 1961, James H. Meredith filed suit in the United States District Court for Southern Mississippi, contending that he had been denied admission to the University of Mississippi solely on racial grounds. In keeping with the 1954 decision, Meredith's right to attend the university was affirmed by a federal district court, confirmed by the Court of Appeals for the Fifth Circuit, and upheld by Justice Hugo Black, speaking with the authority of the United States Supreme Court.

Despite three court orders of the federal government, the university refused to admit Meredith. The governor of the state, Ross Barnett, forbade the university to obey the United States judges. The situation was viewed as the most serious conflict between federal and state authority since the Civil War. Step by step, the federal government tried to bring about Mississippi's compliance with the law. Meredith was turned back in three peaceful attempts to enter.

Time describes the third attempt:

> Meredith, accompanied by John Doar of the Justice Department, went to the door of the office of the state college board.
>
> "Governor Barnett, I'm John Doar of the Justice Department, sir. These papers, Governor, I'd like to present you with these papers." The chief U.S. Marshal tried to hand Barnett a sheaf of court orders.
>
> Barnett said that as a matter of "policy" he could not accept any court orders.
>
> "I want to remind you that the Court of Appeals of the Fifth Circuit entered a temporary restraining order at 8:30 this morning enjoining you from interfering in any way with the registration of James Meredith at the University of Mississippi. We'd like to get on now, Governor, to the business of registering Mr. Meredith."
>
> Barnett's reply was to draw a typewritten sheet from his pocket and read off a "proclamation" addressed to Meredith. To "preserve the peace, dignity and tranquility" of the state, rumbled Barnett, "I hereby finally deny you admission to the University of Mississippi."
>
> "Do you refuse to permit us to come in the door?"

"Yes, sir."

"All right. Thank you."

"I do that politely."

"Thank you. We leave politely."

As the 3 men left the building and walked back to the car, the waiting crowd erupted in gleeful yells. "Goddamn dirty nigger bastard, get out of here and stay out!" [19]

The Justice Department gave up on a fourth attempt to register Meredith when federal marshals accompanying him were called back because of the possibility of "major violence and bloodshed."

On September 28, three days after Governor Barnett blocked Meredith's entry to the college board office, Barnett was found guilty of civil contempt and was ordered by the Court of Appeals to purge himself or face arrest and a fine of ten thousand dollars a day.

The next day President John F. Kennedy, acting at midnight after holding three telephone conversations during the day with Barnett, called Mississippi's National Guard into federal service and dispatched troops of the United States Army to Memphis to stand in reserve in the event more forces were needed. He issued a proclamation calling on the government and the people of Mississippi to "cease and desist" all their obstructing actions and to "disperse and retire peaceably forthwith."

Armed conflict between American soldiers and Mississippi law-enforcement officers and citizens appeared to be almost imminent. But during the day on September 30, Governor Barnett finally agreed to the admission of James Meredith. He also pledged that he would use the forces of the State of Mississippi to maintain order.

That night Meredith was flown from Memphis to Oxford in a federal plane. He was met at the university airport by Deputy Attorney General Nicholas deB. Katzenbach and driven to the campus in a convoy of automobiles and military trucks. Waiting to protect him were three hundred federal marshals, carrying riot clubs and tear-gas cartridges, and a large force of Mississippi state troopers. Governor Barnett, as planned, made a statement indicating that his resistance was over. President Kennedy made a nationally televised address to the nation but aimed directly at the students and people of Mississippi, urging them to comply with the law. But even as the President spoke, rioting raged on the Mississippi campus. The sequence of events was tersely and vividly reported by *Life*:

5:00 P.M. *Sunday.* The federal marshals surround the Lyceum administration building in which Meredith will register. They wear white helmets and orange vests stuffed with tear gas shells. Many carry riot guns. A crowd of hostile students grows across the street yelling "nigger lover" and "two, one, four, three, we hate Kennedy." Meredith arrives at the airport in a border patrol plane. Along the highway from the airport to the university cars of lean, leathery men from the delta are waiting for him. As Meredith passes a shout of "'nigger, nigger" goes up. His calvacade sweeps up to Baxter Hall on the edge of the campus, deposits him and leaves a guard of 24 government marshals there for his safekeeping.
6:00. The crowd on campus is getting close to 2,000 and becoming ugly. Loud screams of "Yankee go home" mix with the piercing rebel yells. Undergraduates in Confederate uniforms strut among the mob. Then attention turns to newsmen. A cameraman is trapped in his car with his wife by angry students and red-necks. The rioters break all his windows, kick in his windshield, push in his hood, smash his camera, burn

his film, and have climbed inside the car to attack his wife before state police finally come to break it up. The mob presses forward again, heaving rocks, spitting and tossing rotten eggs at the marshals around the Lyceum. "God damn nigger-loving bastards," they scream. The lawmen warn them to keep their distance. The mob throws a fire bomb at a federal truck. Suddenly a salvo from the marshal's tear gas guns cuts the air.

7:00. It is dark and people are shouting in the distance. More tear gas guns can be heard in back of the building. Out of the darkness comes a hail of bricks. The marshals fire again and bands of students can be seen running back and forth, disappearing into the gloom.

8:00. The mob is getting stronger. A fire hose splashes out of the black, killing the tear gas. Marshals yell and charge and fire their pistols into the hose to stop the water. Inside the Lyceum building the wounded begin to line the corridors. Broken arms and legs and ankles. Smashed hands and ribs. In a corner one marshal lies in a growing pool of blood, caught in a neck artery with a blast of shotgun pellets. A Department of Justice aide barks into the shortwave radio. "Are we getting medical capability here? Let's get a doctor before this man dies."

9:00. "Gas is getting short," a marshal warns. "The men request permission to return fire." Nicholas Katzenbach, Deputy U.S. Attorney General, furrows his brow, answers calmly. "If you can just hold your fire for a few minutes more," he says. "The President's on the telephone talking to the governor now."

10:00. The cacophony of battle—explosions, shots, crashes, yells—thunders outside. Twelve marshals lie broken and suffering along the blood-spattered corridors inside, nearly obscured now and then in the swirling clouds of tear gas. Others are collapsed, weeping inside their gas masks. The ladies' bathroom is converted into a field hospital.

11:00. A bulldozer leads a new attack on the Lyceum. It rams a tree, reaches the main defense line—University Drive—before it is halted. A marshal comes back to explain: "We got a cannister of gas up there on the three guys running the dozer and knocked them off." But tear gas bombs are growing short. At last some arrive through the back door. Officers frantically break open the wood crates with bayonets and grab handfuls of the black cannisters. A blood-covered red-neck is propelled in the door, guided by two angry marshals who hammer-lock his arms. "Sit down, dynamite," demands one of them. The man acts arrogant. "Don't give me that crap," a marshal shouts. "You're going to get clobbered if you do."

12 Midnight/Monday/. In the Lyceum radios crackle with outgoing messages for help, messages imploring to know the whereabouts of some helicopters that we hear are bringing in Army reinforcements. "We can hold out another 15 or 20 minutes, just get in here," pleads Katzenbach into his microphone.

1:00 A.M. The battle rages on, with snipers added. Four bullets embed themselves in the paneling around the Lyceum's white front door. "Get away from that door," a marshal shouts. "He has us zeroed in." One man who has been zeroed in is Joseph Denson, deputy marshal from Staten Island, N.Y. Two shotgun pellets penetrate his grenade vest, his sport coat, and are slowed only when they finally hit a black wallet he carries containing his identification card.

2:00. Baxter Hall, where Meredith is lodged for the night, and the chemical building, where students are trying to concoct explosives, become new targets for the rioters. Forty marshals join the twenty-four already around Baxter. A few minutes later, the first MPs arrive. Their camouflaged helmets and rifles with bayonets are a reassuring sight.

3:00. A weird and eerie scene, as the soldiers and marshals ring the Lyceum, their weapons pointed skyward. They are immobile as the mob surges toward them and then back, hurling Molotov cocktails and firecrackers. Three autos are on fire. Around the pyres, the rioters can be seen darting back and forth. They scream a scream that curdles the blood— hysterical and shrill, animal. A marshal on the front line turns to a companion and says quietly, "If I were Meredith, I'd be ashamed to go to school with those sorry bastards." Inside the Lyceum command post Howard Reis of the Department of Justice holds an open line to Washington. He hears that fresh troops are moving up Sorority Row toward the Lyceum and University Circle. Brig. General Charles Billingslea, tall, angular, now moves into the post. Katzenbach looks relieved. Tear gas was running dangerously short again.

4:00. General Billingslea and his aides prepare their battle plan. "We'll take the power plant first," they finally decide.

5:00. The mopping up begins. Troops move out slowly from their positions on truck beds and the ground before the Lyceum, their bayonet-tipped rifles carried upward and out. The mob falls back. Another convoy of troops comes up behind them. A Molotov cocktail arcs at the lead jeep. It catches fire and burns brightly. The rebel yells mount.

Inside the Lyceum four prisoners are hustled in. The fourth man in line is thought to be the sniper. As he moves down the hall in handcuffs marshals say "Bastard, bastard." "You never saw the inside of a university before," snarls one. "Start a war will you?" The man is kicked down the hall.

6:00. Dawn. The scene is staggering. The front steps of the Lyceum are covered with ankle-twisting bricks and thousands of empty gas cartridges. Bullet holes form a triangle on the wooden door jamb. In front of the Fine Arts Center three twisted, charred hunks of metal that were cars a few hours before squat crazily in the street, smoking. Chunks of brick and green glass from a thousand pop bottles litter the pavement of University Circle. In low places the tear gas still eddies, causing a sudden smarting of the throat and nose and copious weeping. On a road behind the Lyceum stand the remains of a partial barricade—a stone loveseat, wood, some dormitory furniture.

7:00. It is chilly. The marshals are up from their fitful sleep, eating C rations. The Army is in control. FBI agents are beginning to interrogate the 93 prisoners—only a handful are Ole Miss students—and cataloguing their weapons: a .22 automatic rifle, a Swedish Mauser, an 8-inch auger and a 30-inch length of rubber hose. The prisoners are marched into the interrogation room with their hands clasped behind their heads. Most of them are young, rough-looking punks.

8:00. Meredith is in Registrar Ellis' office being registered. Next he leaves the office. When the TV lights hit him and he sees the horde of newsmen outside he seems to lose composure. For a moment he looks very small and very frightened.

9:00. Meredith and a group of marshals move out the Lyceum's back door. Students begin shouting. It is the familiar, ominous mob voice of the night before, without the rifle fire. Tear gas drives off a phalanx of students trying to head them off. Boys and girls run, dabbing at their eyes. A soft rain begins. Students jeer the tired, uneasy marshals. The rain becomes heavier; the crowd disperses after half-heartedy stoning one more car. The long night is over.[20]

Open warfare was now at an end, but a federal presence remained on campus for several months thereafter, first in the form of a dwindling number of troops, and then marshals. Meredith did graduate from the university and federal authority was upheld, but opposition in nonviolent ways continued to intimidate Meredith throughout his stay.[21]

The episodes of political violence surveyed in this chapter are exceptional and limited kinds of political violence in that they are confined to defiance of federal authority. In many other instances, as we shall see in this book, political factors underlie much of the violence committed against ethnic and economic groups. Again, the elements surrounding social violence are like Maitland's characterization of law, "a seamless webb."

NOTES

1. Arthur M. Schlesinger, "Political Mobs and the American Revolution, 1765–1776," *American Philosophical Society Proceedings*, Vol. XCIX (1955), p. 244. For a comparative study of mobs in England before 1765 which "will enable us to see the material with which the American radicals had to work, and how they used it to further their own programs," see R. S. Longley, "Mob Activities in Revolutionary Massachusetts," *New England Quarterly*, Vol. VI (1933), pp. 99–130. This article also includes a broad and revealing survey of mob activity in the colony before 1765. Another important comparative study is Lloyd I. Rudolph, "The Eighteenth Century Mob in America and Europe," *American Quarterly*, Vol. XI (1959), pp. 447–469. The definitive work on the European mob in George Rude's *The Crowd in History: A Study of Popular Disturbances in France and England, 1730–1848* (New York, 1964).

2. See Gordon S. Wood, "A Note on Mobs in the American Revolution," *William and Mary Quarterly*, Vol. XXIII (1966), pp. 634–642.

3. Bernard Bailyn, ed., *Pamphlets of the American Revolution, 1750–1776*, Vol. I (Cambridge, Massachusetts, 1965), p. 582. For accounts of rioting in the Colonial cities, see Carl Bridenbaugh's *Cities in the Wilderness* (New York, 1955),

pp. 196, 224, 382–383; and *Cities in Revolt* (New York, 1955), pp. 114–118. For studies of agrarian violence, see Irving Mark, *Agrarian Conflicts in Colonial New York, 1711–1775* (New York, 1940), Chapter 4, especially pp. 111–112, 115–116, 124–126; Richard M. Brown, *The South Carolina Regulators* (Cambridge, Massachusetts, 1963), Chapters 1, 2; and Richard J. Hooker, ed., *The Carolina Backcountry on the Eve of the Revolution* (Chapel Hill, 1953).

4. Quoted in Edmund S. Morgan, ed., *Prologue to Revolution* (Chapel Hill, 1959), pp. 106–108. The most important study of the Stamp Act crisis is Edmund S. and Helen M. Morgan, *The Stamp Act Crisis: Prologue to Revolution,* rev. ed. (New York, 1963).

5. See Benjamin W. Labaree, *The Boston Tea Party* (New York, 1964).

6. *Ibid.,* p. 141.

7. *Ibid.,* p. 144.

8. John C. Miller, *Origins of the American Revolution* (Stanford, California, 1966), pp. 296–297.

9. See F. J. Wood, "Paper Money and Shays' Rebellion," *Stone & Webster Journal,* Vol. XXVI (1920), pp. 333–345, 422–434.

10. See Robert E. Moody, "Samuel Ely: Forerunner of Shays," *New England Quarterly,* Vol. V (1932), pp. 105–134.

11. See Jonathan Smith, "The Depression of 1785 and Daniel Shays' Rebellion," *American Antiquarian Society Proceedings,* Vol. XV (1902), pp. 200–232.

12. See Marion L. Starkey, *A Little Rebellion* (New York, 1955).

13. See Millard Hansen, "The Significance of Shays' Rebellion," *South Atlantic Quarterly,* Vol. VI (1933), pp. 99–130.

14. Thomas Jefferson, *Writings,* Paul L. Ford, ed., Vol. VI (New York and London, 1904), p. 64.

15. The only book-length study of this incident is Leland D. Baldwin, *Whiskey Rebels: The Story of a Frontier Uprising* (Pittsburgh, 1939).

16. See Bennett M. Rich, "Washington and the Whiskey Insurrection," *Pennsylavnia Magazine of History and Biography,* Vol. LV (1891), pp. 334–352.

17. *Cf.* Alfred P. James, "A Political Interpretation of the

Whiskey Rebellion," *Western Pennsylvania History Magazine*, Vol. XXXIII (1950), pp. 90–101.

18. See Anthony Lewis, *Portrait of a Decade: The Second American Revolution* (New York, 1964), pp. 214–224. See also L. Still, "Man Behind the Headlines," *Ebony*, Vol. XVIII (December, 1962), pp. 25–28; "Mississippi: The Sound and the Fury," *Newsweek*, Vol. LX (October 15, 1962), pp. 23–29.

19. "Edge of Violence," *Time*, Vol. LXXX (October 5, 1962), p. 21.

20. "Battlefield: Where the Law Won," *Life*, Vol. LIII (October 12, 1962), pp. 32–39.

21. See Lewis, *op. cit.*, p. 221.

5

THE ANTI-CATHOLIC
TRADITION

" 'Blood for blood!' "

America's history of religious bigotry was marked by violence at the very outset of the English settlement. The Puritans persecuted all other religious sects, and in October, 1657, an anti-Quaker law was passed banishing all Quakers from the colony. If a male Quaker should return, one ear was cropped; should he come back a second time, the other ear was removed; and the third time his tongue was to be bored with a hot iron. A woman was whipped for the first two offenses, but for a third, her tongue was to be bored. When these penalties failed to stop them, the death penalty was added the following year for those who returned after banishment.[1]

The epidemic of witchcraft trials in the spring of 1692 in Salem Village remains an awful memory for students of America's past. In this brutal episode more than twenty persons suffered death at the hands of the establishment.

But it was the Catholics who more than any other religious group were the victims of violence stemming from religious bigotry. From the time that Lord Baltimore founded Maryland as a haven for his fellow Catholics through the end of the nineteenth century, violence plagued the lives of American Catholics.

Like commercial panics, periodical outbursts of irreligious fanaticism seem to have become regular incidents in the history of the United States—occurrences to be looked for with as much certainty as if they were the natural outgrowth of our civilization and the peculiarly-constituted condition of American society.[2]

The settlers who came to America from England in the seventeenth century had been reared in an atmosphere of intolerance, and they brought with them to the new land the anti-Popery which characterized the England of that time. Anti-Catholic sentiment in America was so widespread by 1700 that Catholics had no full civil and religious rights anywhere except in Rhode Island, where liberal interpretations of statutes made life bearable for them. The outbreak of war between England and Catholic France in 1689, and again in 1701, with France and Spain as allies, made all Catholics suspect as potential enemies whose papal allegiance might supersede their loyalty to the English crown, resulting in their cooperation with the armies of French Canada and Spanish Florida against the settlers. Americans felt the same Catholic threat against their national existence that the English had felt in the days of Elizabeth.[3]

During the first two decades of the new republic the anti-Catholic tradition generally took nonviolent, subtle forms. However, once the number of Catholics began to grow significantly as a result of a high birth rate and increasing immigration, the hostility came to the surface, so that by the 1830's the traditional violent patterns began to reappear.

One of the earliest incidents of this renewed anti-Catholic violence was the destruction of a Catholic school run by an order of Ursuline nuns in Charlestown, Massachusetts, in 1834. Most of the pupils were girls from affluent Protestant families who were attracted to the convent because of its reputation for high educational standards. The local Protestant sects, led by their clergy, resented the success of the school. A trumped-up scandal was publicized in the Boston press which aroused a mob to such a pitch of fury against "Popery and nunneries" that they burned and looted the establishment, leaving it a mass of charred ruins.

On the evening of the 11th, knots of half a dozen or a dozen men were seen, about half past eight o'clock, gathering in the neighborhood of the Nunnery. Soon after this a cart laden with tar barrels and other combustibles passed to the spot. This showed that burning was premeditated, and soon the work began. The doors and windows of the Nunnery were soon broken in by stones and other missiles, and a beacon fire was kindled, apparently as a signal to other rioters, upon the hill. The crowd quickly increased to a multitude. It was certain that this was a preconcerted movement; for the burning of the tar barrels was a signal for assembling, among the mass of citizens which would be collected, a large number who had entered into a combination for the destruction of the Convent.

A party of fifty to a hundred persons, or perhaps more, disguised by fantastic dresses and painted faces, after warning the inmates, who had all retired to rest, by wild noises and threats of violence, to make their escape, proceeded to make an active assault upon the house. The ladies of the institution, alarmed by these threats of violence, immediately took the children under their charge, and with them retired from the rear of the house to the garden, and made their escape to some of the neighboring dwellings. The assailants pressed the evacuation of the house with such haste, that it is said they laid violent hands upon the Lady Superior to hasten her movements. The distress and terror of the scene were heightened by the solicitude of the nuns for one of their number, who was confined to her bed of a disease which she was not expected to recover from. The assailants forced open the doors and windows of the Convent, carried most of the furniture, among which were three piano-fortes, a harp, and other musical instruments, into the yard, and there destroyed it. As they applied the torch, the fragments, as the flames spread through the building, were again thrown on to feed the fire. At about half past twelve o'clock they set fire to the building in the second story, and in a short time it was entirely destroyed.

A great number of persons were assembled at the spot, and were witnesses of the proceedings; and it was impossible to tell them, as it is now, why no measures were taken to repress them. It could not be learned that any magistrates or police officers came upon the ground. Several fire companies from Boston, Charlestown, and Cambridge repaired to the scene on the first alarm, and, when they ascertained the cause of it, a part of them returned home. A number of the fire companies, however, were present during the conflagration; and the effectual measures which were taken to suppress it appear to have been overcome by the great number of persons assembled, many of them evidently from a distance, for the apparent purpose of encouraging and aiding in the work of destruction.

Besides the Nunnery, several other buildings belonging to the establishment were also burned. The fire was deliberately communicated to the chapel, to the bishop's lodge, the stables, and the old nunnery—a large wooden building situated at a short distance from the others. The work of destruction was continued until daylight, when the mob dispersed. The pecuniary value of the property destroyed was not estimated at the time. It was from fifty to a hundred thousand dollars, and was insured, on building and furniture, for about sixteen thousand dollars.

The accounts further stated that the firemen of Charlestown looked on in silence, without attempting to extinguish the flames, and the Boston department were compelled by violence to abstain from all efforts to put out the fire or save the property. Everything was burned with the utmost deliberation, and without the slightest sentiment in opposition to the insanity of the mob. To crown the proceedings with an appropriate conclusion, the tomb at the foot of the gardens was entered, the coffins robbed of the plates bearing the names of the persons who lie buried there, and one of the coffins broken open, and its relics exposed. Even up to the next day there was not a single officer upon the spot to protect the remains of the dead from violation and insult. . . .

A very large number of young fellows, less than twenty-one years of age, were mixed in with the mob, and joined in the proceedings, with all the recklessness of unrestrained youth when engaged in a "row" where there were none to withhold them. The religious character of the place was a special mark for their profane irreverence and ribald jests, and all sought to outdo each other in mad pranks and prurient specimens of blackguardism. . . .

The commotion among the Roman Catholics was immense. Proclamations were issued by the Governor of Massachusetts and the Mayor of Boston in regard to keeping the peace; the Charlestown Selectmen offered a large reward for the apprehension of the leaders of the riot, and the military was kept in arms in Boston, for some time, through fear of an outbreak. This was more than thirty-five years ago; and nothing similar to this sensation, either in character or dimensions, has since occurred among us.[4]

When Irish laborers employed on construction work in surrounding towns heard of the convent's destruction, they made plans to hurry to Boston on a mission of revenge. Priests were immediately sent out to intercept the infuriated Irishmen and instruct them to go back and not "raise a finger."[5]

The trial of the rioters resulted in the acquittal of all those who had been arrested for arson. The ringleader was acquitted in spite of conclusive evidence against him, and he walked out of court with the cheers of the spectators ringing in his ears.

All through the 1830's forces had been at work to increase animosity toward the Catholics in America: societies, newspapers, magazines, churches, and a political party were all enlisted in the cause. Extraordinary intolerance had been instilled in thousands of people. The old anti-Catholic hatred, the fear of economic competition from the swelling number of Irish immigrant laborers, and the threat of increasing political power as more and more Catholics went to the polls were all factors in the situation.

The decade covered by the thirties is unique in our history. Fifty years of life at high pressure had brought the people to a state of excitement, of lawlessness, of mob rule, such as had never before existed. Intolerance, turbulence, riot, became the order of the day. Appeals were made not to reason but to force; reforms, ideas, institutions that were not liked were attacked and put down by violence; and one of the least liked and first to be assaulted was the Church of Rome.[6]

Beyond the thirties into the forties, the prejudice against Catholicism or "Popery" inevitably led to violence and bloodshed because the depth of feeling created by anti-Catholic agitators demanded physical expression at some point.[7] That point reached a climax in Philadelphia during the spring of 1844 when American "natives" and Irish Catholic "foreigners" clashed in a series of riots which turned the City of Brotherly Love into a chaos charged with hatred and violence.

A few months before the violent outbreaks which erupted in May, there was a raging controversy in the city concerning the reading of the Protestant Bible in the public schools. Bishop Kenrick of the diocese of Philadelphia had petitioned the school board to permit Catholic children to use the Catholic version. The local Native American party and Protestant ministers aroused the public at meetings by claiming that the Catholics wanted to prevent Protestant children from reading their own Bible. The issue raged throughout the city, and rallies and demonstrations were the order of the day.

On May 3 the Native Americans, a new third political party which had been organized the year before to house the enemies of Catholics and foreigners in general, arranged to hold a street rally in the Irish Kensington district in Philadelphia. The very presence of the Natives was a provocation, and enraged Irishmen broke up the meeting. Driven from their meeting, the remnants of the Natives met in a safe place elsewhere and passed a resolution calling for another public rally at the same spot in Kensington on May 6.

The proceedings were violent in language against the Irish, but not in acts, till a storm of rain compelled those assembled to seek refuge in a neighboring market-house. In the rush, collisions took place, blows were struck, and fire-arms used. The meeting continued and finally closed. But at ten o'clock at night, the Native Americans gathered a mob and began an attack on the houses occupied by Irish families. The inmates fled, and the mob, after destroying all they could, set fire to the buildings, which were soon consumed. Some attempt was made by those attacked to defend their lives and property, and here the first of the rioters was slain. Then the cry was raised: "To the nunnery!" A rush was made by the mob, and the house which had been occupied by a little community endeavoring to organize like Sisters of Charity was next attacked by the Native Americans, but a volley from a few defenders drove them off for a time. The riot thus far had resulted in the death and wounding of several and the wanton destruction of property.[8]

By the next day the whole city was caught in the grip of violence. The local party press editorialized:

> Our columns are shrouded in black to-day to commemorate one of the most infernal violations of freedom and the rights of man, that has ever been perpetrated in this land. The hirelings of George III in our early troubles, are thrown into the shade, in point of outrage, by the violent and deadly conduct of the Catholics of Kensington. We have not language to describe their enormity.

> Another St. Bartholomew's day is begun in the streets of Philadelphia. The bloody hand of the Pope has stretched itself forth to our destruction. We now call on our fellow-citizens to arm.[9]

A meeting was called by the Native Americans at 3 P.M. that day at the State House yard, and all followers were advised to be prepared for defense. Earlier in the day a procession paraded the streets with an American flag on which were inscribed the words, "This is the flag that was trampled upon by the Irish papists." Along the way two Irishmen were grabbed by a group of Natives who recognized them as rioters from the previous night. They were taken to an alderman's home to be charged.

> So intense was the excitement of the people, who surrounded these men on their way to the office, that it was with the greatest difficulty that violent hands were kept from their persons. The cry of the people was, "Kill them, kill them! Blood for blood!" Every moment those men were in the streets—and they hurried with great precipitation—it was thought they would be forcibly dragged from the hands of Mr. Allburger, and sacrificed in the public street, to satiate the vengeance of an outraged people.[10]

A mass meeting was held at the State Yard, with most of the participants armed to the hilt. Resolutions were passed denouncing the "gross and atrocious outrage" of what happened the day before in Kensington, and "considering the Bible in the public schools as necessary to a faithful course of instruction therein."

The mob then moved on to Kensington. Crossing the Irish section, they shouted insults and began to attack the Hibernia Hose Company,

> . . . which was soon destroyed, with its contents; and the houses inhabited by Irish people were set on fire, till twenty-nine, and the neighboring market, were in flames.
>
> Such was the condition of affairs when the First Brigade, and two companies of the Third Brigade, under General

Cadwalader, appeared on the scene, and further violence was prevented, but the fire department made no effort to save the burning houses.

The next day a mob gathered at St. Michael's Church, and about two o'clock Captain Fairlamb, in command of detachment of militia, demanded of Rev. William Loughran, the pastor, the keys of the church and the pastoral residence. Finding that there was no one there to defend it, the military, instead of protecting the church, allowed three of the mob to enter the church and set it on fire. The house was then broken into, the furniture demolished, and the house fired.[11]

The spreading fire destroyed ten other houses in the area. Later in the afternoon the mob moved toward St. Augustine's Church on Fourth Street.

Here some show of protection was made. Mayor Scott stationed the city watch in front, and took up his position in the rear with a posse of citizens. Undeterred by these, the mob gathered, and in a short time an attack was made with bricks, stones, and other missiles. The Mayor was knocked down senseless, and the watch and posse was scattered.[12]

At this point the First City Troops arrived, but they made no effort to disperse the mob. The church was by now on fire. When the fire enveloped the base of the cupola, "the sight was hailed by a loud cheer," and when the cross fell into the street, another cheer resounded.[13] An eyewitness described the scene:

It was but a few minutes after the match had been applied, when the whole edifice was a mass of flames, the fire, bursting from the many windows, licked the walls and mounted to the cupola. High above the billows of the fiery sea shone the glittering emblem of salvation; for minutes it swayed in the torrid atmosphere, then with a far-sounding crash fell into its translucent grave. A yell as of twice twenty thousand savages greeted the fall of the Cross, while a witnessing Israelite, with biting sarcasm remarked, "I did not know there [were] so many Jews in Philadelphia." [14]

Martial law was finally declared on the night of May 8, and with this the mobs finally dispersed. But within a month, on July 4, the excitement accompanying Independence Day led to clashes between Irish laborers and a group of American Natives. Rumors were spread about the city that the Church of Saint Philip de Neri in another suburb contained arms.

On Friday, the 5th of July, it was learned that an attack would be made on St. Philip Neri's Church. This time the authorities were more active. Militia were ordered to the scene, but the rioters, having secured two cannon, broke into the church, which they attempted to set on fire after dislodging the small force of soldiers. A part of the first division, under General Cadwalader arrived in time to save the building; but the mob attacked the soldiery, so that a regular battle ensued, cannon and small arms being used on both sides. Several were killed and wounded, but the rioters were finally dispersed, and though they gathered again on Monday were at last overawed.[15]

When at last the city took an accounting of the period of rioting and mob rule, it found that more than a dozen citizens had been killed and at least fifty had been wounded in three days of fighting. There was little sense of remorse. Official investigations placed the blame for the riots on the Irish exclusively. But at least for the time being, the violence shocked much of the rest of the country, and the American Republican party, an outgrowth of the original Native American party, faded away as a result.

But not too many years passed before the anti-Catholic Know-Nothing, or American, party became a major political force in the country from 1850 through 1859. Its aim was to eliminate Catholics from every sector of American life, if not deport them back to Ireland. By 1855 it controlled a number of state legislatures and had a large enough representation in Congress to hold a balance-of-power position for a brief period of time.[16]

The party encouraged violence in American politics, and the period of the 1850's was charged with election day riots. The Know-Nothing clubs were pledged to keep Catholics and foreign-born citizens from voting, and the Democratic organizations were determined to protect these groups at the polls. Police were useless when these clashes took place, and sensible citizens stayed home rather than risk their lives in the pitched battles that developed around every polling place.[17] Baltimore was particularly bad, and events there in the municipal election in 1856 can exemplify the story in most American cities at that time. Excerpts from the diary of a local citizen give a good idea of the situation:

October 8. This has been one of the most disgraceful days for Baltimore. From early in the morning until very late at night, both parties have been drawn in deadly array against each other, and Plug Uglies and Rip Raps and Eighth Ward Blackguards have endeavoured to see which could be vilest and most inhuman. The so-called American party seems to have the most villainous material in its composition, while the other side has never been deficient in that article. A number of men have been killed to-day and over fifty wounded, more or less dangerously.

October 9. The day is bright and beautiful, but the evil passions of men seem not yet to have died out. Fights and wounds of various kinds were the order of the day, and on a small scale some of the scenes of yesterday were re-enacted.[18]

During the interval between this and the Presidential election, attempts were made to assure a peaceful election on November 4 by having troops in readiness to take care of any eruptions which the city officials were fearful would take place.

The events of the day proved that the fears were not ill founded. Fighting and rioting occurred in various parts of the city, but the most serious affair was in and around Belair Market. The fighting here began about three o'clock and continued desperately until dark. The Know-Nothings brought with them a small cannon mounted on wheels, which was loaded with all kinds of missiles. The Democrats, however, overpowered them and got possession of the cannon, and the high constable and twenty policemen were not able to prevent the rioters from carrying it off. As a result of this fighting we find a list of ten killed and over two hundred and fifty wounded, making a total of fourteen killed in the two elections.[19]

In practically every American city the same state of affairs prevailed. The speakers and publications produced by the Know-Nothings brought to the surface native Protestant prejudice against the Irish Catholics, and rioting in city after city took place during this decade of the 1850's.

One of the most violent of all the riots began on election day, August 7, 1854, in St. Louis, Missouri. A rumor that all Catholic churches were arsenals once again brought mobs to one of the churches. The incident which was said to have triggered what followed was the stabbing in the back of an American by an Irishman. It was usual to charge the Irish with starting arguments. In any event, it suited the purpose. A mob ransacked steamboats at the wharf, supplied itself with axes and other implements, and looted and hacked whole rows of houses in which the Irish lived. Of course the Irish fought back.

> For forty-eight hours the city has been the scene of one of the most appalling riots that has ever taken place in the country. Men have been butchered like cattle; property destroyed and anarchy reigns supreme. . . . The military and police have, thus far, been unable to check the onward march of lawlessness and crime. The scenes of last night were terrible, never, we hope to be enacted again.[20]

Eight to ten persons were estimated to have been killed, thirty seriously wounded, and a large number injured.

Almost a year later on election day, August 6, 1855, in Louisville, Kentucky, a mob brandishing bowie knives and muskets and pulling a brass cannon attempted to ravage a Catholic church, but was dissuaded by the mayor. The mob did, however, attack the Irish quarter, burning down houses and killing at least twenty persons. The event is still remembered as "Bloody Monday."

It was the Civil War which finally brought about the decline of the American Party, or Know-Nothings, as a political force, and with it the end of anti-Catholic legislation as well as the violence of the mobs. But one of the main reasons for the end of *organized* persecution of the Catholics at this time was that various groups were turning their attention to extirpating the Mormon practice of polygamy. Indeed, the Mormons had their share of religious persecution during their early history, some of it coinciding with the victimization of the Irish Catholics. It should also be noted that the Catholics continued to be victims of America's religious bigotry through the end of the nineteenth century. The form of this enduring bigotry was not physical violence, but it was no less a violation of human dignity.

NOTES

1. See William W. Sweet, *Religion in Colonial America* (New York, 1942), pp. 144–153.
2. "Anti-Catholic Movement in the United States," *Catholic World,* Vol. X (1875), p. 810.
3. See Ray A. Billington, *The Protestant Crusade* (Gloucester, Massachusetts, 1963), p. 4. This is the finest study of the history of anti-Catholic and antiforeign sentiment in the United States. The documentation is overwhelming: 1,548 notes (mostly from primary sources) to 316 pages of text.
4. Quoted in *The Charlestown Convent: Its Destruction by a Mob on the Night of August 11, 1834; with a History of the Excitement before the Burning, and the Strange and Exaggerated Reports Relating Thereto, the Feeling of Regret and Indignation Afterwards; the Proceedings of Meetings, and Expressions of the Contemporary Press* (Boston, 1870), pp. 33–35.
5. See Gustavus Myers, *History of Bigotry in the United States* (New York, 1943), Chapter 9.
6. John B. McMaster, *With the Fathers* (New York, 1896), p. 71.
7. See Billington, *op. cit.,* pp. 220–221.
8. John D. Shea, *History of the Catholic Church in the United States,* Vol. IV (New York, 1886–1898), p. 48.

9. *The Native American,* May 7, 1844.
10. *Ibid.,* May 8, 1844.
11. Shea, *op. cit.,* p. 50.
12. *Ibid.*
13. United States *Gazette,* May 9, 1844.
14. "The Anti-Catholic Riots of 1844 in Philadelphia," *American Catholic Historical Researchers,* Vol. XII (1896), pp. 55–56.
15. Shea, *op. cit.,* pp. 53–54.
16. See Billington, *op. cit.,* p. 234.
17. See *ibid.,* p. 421; and Carleton Beals, *Brass-Knuckle Crusade* (New York, 1960).
18. Quoted in Laurence F. Schmeckebier, *History of the Know-Nothing Party in Maryland,* Johns Hopkins University Studies in History and Political Science, Vol. XVII (Baltimore, 1899), p. 38.
19. *Ibid.,* p. 41.
20. See Beals, *op. cit.,* Chapter 9.

6

MORMONS AND THE NATION

*. . . a "mobocrat" answered, "Nits make lice,"
and blew out his brains.*

When Mark Twain said of the Mormons, "Their religion is singular but their wives are plural," he was probably expressing the sum of what was, and still is, generally known about them. It might be useful, then, to trace something of the history of this religious group, which perhaps more than any other sect endured violent oppression at the hands of fellow American citizens.[1]

The Mormon Church was founded in the early 1830's, a decade in which the rise of many strange sects reflected the desire of the rootless American frontier society for some sense of purpose in life and some sense of community. What made Mormonism so attractive in this turbulent society was Joseph Smith's magnetic leadership and his claim to infallibility through direct conversation with the Almighty. He confirmed the popular belief that the signs of the times indicated the end was imminent, and proclaimed the formation of a new society exclusively fit to receive the Messiah on His return. In the language of the sect, the Saints, as they called themselves to distinguish Mormons from the unregenerate "Gentiles," were to be "gathered to Zion."

The early history of the Mormons is the story of their wanderings in search of Zion. So zealous were the proselytes of this new faith that church membership increased with amazing rapidity, in some cases whole congregations converting at once. Caught up in the westward movement of the time, the church transferred its headquarters to Kirtland, Ohio, near the shore of Lake Erie, a little east of Cleveland.

From here they branched out in 1831 to Independence, Jackson County, Missouri, which was on the extreme western frontier of that time. They settled on land purchased from the federal government which was consecrated by Smith as a site for the New Jerusalem, a "Stake of Zion," thus setting it apart as their inheritance. Native Missourians felt threatened both politically and economically by this professed belief.[2] They were determined to take the law into their own hands and drive the Mormons out. What aroused them most was the Saints' apparent opposition to slavery and their alleged invitations to free blacks and mulattoes to settle there.

After several Mormon houses and farms had been shot at and burned, a mob of native Missourians met on July 18, 1838, and issued a "manifesto" demanding the ouster of the alien religionists:

> We, the undersigned, citizens of Jackson County, believing that an important crisis is at hand as regards our civil society, in consequence of a pretended religious sect of people that

have settled and are settling in our country, styling themselves as Mormons, and intending as we do to rid our society "peaceably if we can, forcibly if we must"; and believing as we do that the arm of the civil law does not afford us a guarantee or at least a sufficient one against the evils which are now inflicted upon us, and seem to be increasing by the said religious sect, deem it expedient, and of the highest importance, to form ourselves into a company for the better and easier accomplishment of our purpose, a purpose which we deem it almost superfluous to say, is justified as well by the law of nature, as by the law of self-preservation. . . .

. . . their conduct here stamps their character in their true colors. More than a year since it was ascertained that they had been tampering with our slaves and endeavoring to sow dissensions and raise seditions among them. . . . In a late number of the *Star*, published in Independence by the leaders of the sect, there is an article inviting free Negroes and mulattoes from other states to become Mormons, and remove and settle among us. This exhibits them in still more odious odors. . . .[3]

A committee was sent to the leading members of the church, demanding immediate suspension of the newspaper and immediate expulsion of the Mormons from the county. Church leaders asked for three months in which to consider the demand. This was denied. They then asked for ten days and were advised that they could have fifteen minutes. The leaders of course could not meet this deadline, and the mob proceeded to destroy the presses of the newspaper plant. After they were assured that the Mormons would get out within a day, the mob turned to personal violence. They took the bishop of the church and one other follower and stripped, tarred, and feathered them before a crowd in front of the courthouse. Other Mormons were whipped until they were unconscious. For days unrestrained mobs rode through the countryside, pillaging and burning Mormon property. Mormons organized for defense and this provoked their enemies to greater atrocities.

Both sides appealed to state officials to support them, and caught in the middle as they were, these officials failed to keep the peace. For at least the next five years violence prevailed in the situation in Missouri. A tragic culmination came in October, 1838, when a band of Missourians struck at a settlement known as Haun's Mill. Some of the Mormons fled toward the woods and took shelter in the brush, but one group, including a number of children, hid in the old blacksmith shop. Eighteen in this group were killed and the rest seriously wounded. When one small boy begged for his life, a "mobocrat" answered, "Nits make lice," and blew out his brains.[4] That expression was echoed twenty years later on the hillside at Mountain Meadows in Utah, where the Mormons bloodied their own hands in an episode of not unexpected retaliation.

Feeling in Missouri became so intense that whole areas were in a state of civil war. Governor Boggs, while petitioned by both sides for support and protection, took his stand firmly against the Mormons. In October, 1838, he issued his extermination order: "The Mormons must be treated as enemies, and *must be exterminated or driven from the State* for the public peace."[5] Following the surrender of Joseph Smith and other Mormon leaders, General Lucas tried them by court-martial and sentenced them to be shot for treason in the public square at Far

West. The man commissioned to carry out the order defied his superior officer and got away with it. The order was not carried out.

Forced to find another home, the Mormons settled at Nauvoo, a mosquito-infested bog on the bank of the Mississippi River in Illinois. In five years they transformed it into a busy and prosperous town, the center of a rich farming district; a printing press was set up, a temple begun, and a municipal university projected. With a population of fifteen thousand, it was the largest city in the state. Through bitter experience Joseph Smith had learned to protect his people under the law, so he secured for his city a charter which made it almost independent of the state and which gave it an army for its protection.

But the very prosperity of Nauvoo carried with it the seeds of trouble. The Mormons were already too numerous to suit their enemies, and their numbers were increasing every day. They voted as a bloc, playing the Whigs and Democrats against each other for favors, and eventually aroused the ill will of both. Smith himself aspired to be President of the United States, sending his missionaries out to campaign for him as well as to preach. All this had encouraged stronger opposition to the Mormons from outside the community, and now there was dissension and division from within. Some members who were not in line with the leaders had been excommunicated, and defiantly established a newspaper, the Nauvoo *Expositor*, which attacked Joseph Smith so harshly that he, as mayor of the city, pronounced it a nuisance and ordered it destroyed. Public reaction was instant and violent. Mormon leaders from both factions were arrested and housed in the jail at Carthage, Illinois, under promise of protection, to await trial. Unwilling to await judicial process, a mob gathered about the jail, their fury mounting until they attacked the prison cell and killed Joseph Smith and his brother, Hyrum.[6] Thus June 27, 1844, climaxed more than eleven years of strife between the Mormons and their neighbors of the western frontier.

To the disappointment of their enemies, the Mormons did not scatter but rather resolved to work all the harder and to carry out Smith's plans and to maintain his "kingdom." Their enemies set out to drive them from Illinois. They organized a series of raids upon Mormon homes, drove out farm stock, destroyed furniture, and burned the houses down after warning the families to get out.

The Mormons pleaded for their rights as American citizens, and the natives appealed to have their state rid of the Mormon menace. By October, 1845, Brigham Young, successor to the martyred Joseph Smith, agreed to move his people en masse in the spring. The natives agreed to leave the Mormons alone until then.

But a cruel whim took hold of the natives, and the burnings promptly began anew; the religious community left Nauvoo almost immediately thereafter and obtained temporary respite by settling across the Mississippi in Sugar Creek, Iowa. After some two years of settlement in temporary camps widely scattered in Iowa, Brigham Young led a band of pioneers in the spring of 1847 to select a permanent home for his people. In July, 1847, he decided upon the valley of the Great Salt Lake.

Within a few years towns and villages were established throughout the valley. By 1850 a territorial government

was set up for Utah, with Brigham Young appointed as
governor and with three other Mormons and six Gentiles
completing the official personnel. From the beginning most
of the federally appointed officers from the outside met
with difficulties in Utah.[7] They resented the unquestioning
allegiance of the members of the church to Brigham Young,
which made him in fact the ruler. On the other hand the
people viewed the government appointees with suspicion.
Life in the territory was so difficult for them that one after
another of the officials returned to the states, bearing
reports that pictured the Mormons as insubordinate and
traitorous.

Beyond this, friction continued between the Mormons
and the American public. The coincidence of their having
established themselves at a geographical nodal point in the
Rockies which could not easily be bypassed by immigrants
to either northern or southern California made it inevitable
that their precious isolation would be intruded upon as
the economic importance of the Pacific coast increased.

On July 24, 1857, the Mormons had assembled to
celebrate the tenth anniversary of their arrival in Zion.
Just as the celebration reached its climax, word came
that an army was en route to Utah to "quell the Mormon
rebellion." A state of siege was proclaimed and preparations were made for violent resistance. Of course almost
since the arrival of the Mormons, Gentile wagon trains
on their way to California had been passing through Salt
Lake City and the Mormon country without disturbance.
Several Gentile immigrant trains were in the Mormon
country when this conflict between the United States government and the Mormons gave promise of breaking out

into armed conflict. One of these companies, the Fancher party, had passed through Salt Lake City sometime between July 20 and August 5 and had reached a spot known as Mountain Meadows in southern Utah on or about September 6.

That same evening a special meeting of selected Nauvoo Legion and Mormon Church leaders was held at Cedar City after the regular Sunday services. A decision was reached that the Fancher party should be destroyed, if possible by inciting the Indians to do the job. Indians (probably assisted by some Mormons) did assemble and attack the train, which, however, managed to defend itself. On September 10 a group of Mormon men, organized as a military unit, went to the scene of the attack, approached the Fancher train under the guise of peace, arranged a truce, and gave assurances that if the members of the party would submit to their specific plan of march they would be protected from the Indians and escorted to safety in Cedar City. Eighteen young children were escorted in another group, the adult males were lined up in single file with a Mormon guard on each side, and the train set out. At a signal prearranged among the Mormons and Indians, all except the eighteen children were massacred in cold blood.[8]

"THE BALLAD OF THE MOUNTAIN MEADOWS MASSACRE"

Come, all you sons of liberty,
Unto my rhyme give ear,
'Tis of a bloody massacre,
You presently shall hear.

In splendor o'er the mountains,
Some thirty wagons came,
They were awaited by a wicked band.
O Utah, where's thy shame!

On a crisp October morning
At the Mountain Meadows green
By the light of bright campfires
Lee's Mormon bullets screamed.

In Indian colors all wrapped in shame,
This bloody crew was seen
To flock around this little train,
All on the meadows green.

They were attacked in the morning
As they were on their way.
They forthwith corralled their wagons,
And fought in blood array.

Till came the captain of the band,
He surely did deceive,
Saying, "If you will give up your arms,
We'll surely let you live."

When once they had give up their arms,
Thinking their lives to save,
The words were broken among the rest
Which sent them to their graves.

When once they had give up their arms,
They started for Cedar City.
They rushed on them in Indian style.
O what a human pity!

They melted down with one accord
Like wax before the flame,
Both men and women, old and young.
O Utah, where's thy shame!

Both men and women, old and young,
A-rolling in their gore,
And such an awful sight and scene,
Was ne'er beheld before!

Their property was divided
Among this bloody crew,
And Uncle Sam is bound to see
This bloody matter through.

The soldier will be stationed
Throughout this Utah land,
All for to find those murders out,
And bring them to his hand.

By order from their president
This bloody deed was done.
He was the leader of the Mormon Church,
His name was Brigham Young.[9]

The Mountain Meadows Massacre long remained a stain on the Mormon reputation, but in recent years the sect has officially acknowledged responsibility for it. But the church does remind other religious groups of their own historical record of violence against unbelievers and also properly points out that Mormons were much more the oppressed than the oppressors.

Religious violence in other nations at other times far

exceeds anything ever experienced in the United States. However, as we have stated, religious bigotry, expressed in subtle and sophisticated ways, is surely a violation of human dignity and is as destructive as physical violence. This has certainly characterized the American religious experience.

NOTES

1. For a useful survey of the historical literature dealing with the Mormons, see M. S. Hill, "Historiography of Mormonism," *Church History*, Vol. XXVIII (1959), pp. 418–426.

2. See G. Homer Durham, "Political Interpretations of Mormon History, *Pacific Historical Review*, Vol. XIII (1944), pp. 136–150; and Richard T. Fly, "Econmic Aspects of Mormonism," *Harper's Magazine*, Vol. CVI (1903), pp. 667–678.

3. Quoted in William A. Linn, *The Story of the Mormons* (New York, 1963), p. 170.

4. Quoted in Juanita Brooks, *The Mountain Meadows Massacre* (Norman, Oklahoma, 1962), p. 5. Much of the material in this chapter is drawn from this study. While the author, Juanita Brooks, proudly indicates her Mormon association in the introduction, her book is one of the most reliable and readable works on Mormonism, especially in connection with the Mountain Meadows episode.

5. Linn, *op. cit.*, p. 205.

6. The facts relating to Smith's murder remain in dispute, and no universally acceptable account has appeared even at this late date.

7. For an account of relations between the Mormons and the

federal government, see Leland Creer, *Utah and the Nation* (New York, 1929).

8. See Brooks, *op. cit.*, p. 4.

9. Austin E. Fife, "A Ballad of the Mountain Meadows Massacre," *Western Folklore*, Vol. XII (1953), pp. 229–241.

THE ANTI-CHINESE MOVEMENT

"The crowd appeared maddened
with the taste of blood . . ."

The problem has two aspects. The one is racial, the other economic.

Behind the race antipathy exhibited on the Pacific coast there is a sound feeling. In this country we already have one serious race problem. The presence of the negroes in the South has caused civil war, the one great failure of our judicial system, and the most extravagant of our governmental disasters. We want no second race problem until we have either solved the first, or made it clear that we can solve the second. The solution of neither race problem is within sight. If, after the experience of one such problem, the American people should admit another, by opening undiscriminately their doors to the East, they would be unpardonable.

Behind the economic antipathy to Oriental laborers there is also a justifiable feeling. . . . certainly if there is any body of laborers against which the working people of America need protection, it is the coolie labor of Asia. The fact that the Japanese and Chinese laborers enter industries in which there is a scarcity of whites does not affect the case, for it is not the direct loss of jobs, but the lowering—or at least the changing—of the standards of living that brings injury to the mass.[1]

Such was pretty much the prevailing attitude in the United States toward the Oriental population in the nation which first came to the country during the period beginning with the discovery of gold in California in 1849. By 1852 there were about twenty-five thousand Orientals on the Pacific coast, and they came at the rate of four thousand a year. In the 1860's, because of the demand for laborers on the Central Pacific Railroad, the number grew tremendously. By the end of the seventies there were almost a hundred and fifty thousand Chinese in California alone. Public resentment of the Chinese along the Pacific coast began to stir in the mid-1860's. Their lower standard of living and their willingness to work long hours at relatively low wages were viewed as a serious menace to native labor; and their adherence to the Chinese customs and religion, their exotic appearance and language, aroused racial prejudice.

> Of all stupid ill-feelings, the sentiment of my fellow-Cau-
> casians towards our companions in the Chinese car was the
> most stupid and the worst. They seemed never to have looked
> at them, listened to them, or thought of them, but hated them
> *a priori*. The Mongols were their enemies in that cruel and
> treacherous battlefield of money. They could work better and
> cheaper in half a hundred industries, and hence there was no
> calumny too idle for the Caucasians to repeat, and even to
> believe. They declared them hideous vermin and affected a
> kind of choking in the throat when they beheld them.[2]

Just as the labor of the black man made possible the clearing and development of America's South and West, so Oriental labor contributed greatly to the growth of the

Pacific coast: the Chinese helped construct railroads, wagon roads, and irrigating ditches; and they helped establish profitable factories, canneries, vineyards, and orchards. But this made little enough impression on most of the native inhabitants and certainly did not overcome the economic resentment and racial hatred which gave rise to the violence committed against the "yellow peril."[3]

Los Angeles was the scene in 1871 of a massacre in which a mob of five hundred "Angels," enraged over the killing of a white by some local Chinese in the course of an intra-Chinese tong war, stormed through the Chinese ghetto, leaving eighteen Chinese dead in its wake—fifteen of them hanging from makeshift gallows. A nineteenth victim died from bullet wounds several days after the riot. Besides the slaughter, the Chinese quarters were heavily looted.[4]

Of course Los Angeles itself was at that time a primitive and undeveloped town, allegedly having a "larger percentage of bad characters than any other city" in the country. Estimates of killings in the early fifties ran close to thirty a month, and as late as 1870 one of the local newspapers could announce, "All quiet—No murders or suicides occurred in Los Angeles yesterday."[5] Except for a rare dedicated sheriff, the police force was useless to the citizens and could hardly be distinguished from the criminal element. Vigilante activities substituted the law of the noose for the law of the courts since for all practical purposes law enforcement did not exist. On one occasion in 1855 the mayor of the city temporarily resigned his office to lead a lynch mob.[6]

In such a social climate it might be concluded that the

murdering and looting which characterized the October 24, 1871, episode reflected a general lawlessness as much as a racist sentiment. A local newspaper offered the following account of the event:

Yesterday evening about half past 5 o'clock the quarrel, which has been brewing for some days past, between the Chinese companies in this city, and which caused the shooting affair between Yo Hing and Ah Choy, on Monday, culminated in a shooting affray in Negro Alley between the Chinamen. When the first shot was fired in this affair, our reporter was near at hand and arrived on the scene of action in time to see officers Jesus Bilderrain, Sepulveda, and Esteban Sanchez, and several others rush in and separate the combatants. Hardly had this been done when the Chinamen commenced an indiscriminate firing, shooting every man in sight. One old heathen who didn't seem to be taking a hand in the affair, was no sooner approached and advised to get into a house out of the way of bullets which swept through the air in all directions, then he pulled a six-shooter from under his coat and discharged every barrel at persons in his immediate vicinity. Two others, one of whom is said to have been identified as Ah Choy, stood on the porch in front of Coronel Block, and emptied their pistols at the crowd, which attracted by the firing, had assembled on Los Angeles and Arcadia streets. After twenty-five or thirty shots had been fired, and officer Bilderrain was still in existence, and suggested that those members present repair to the headquarters of the organization. It was recommended that a strong guard be placed around the building, firing, so far as practicable, discontinued and the place stormed by daylight. The excitement intensified and the authorities were powerless to act, the crowd treating commands, entreaties and expostulations with disdain and refusing to listen. At about a quarter to 9 o'clock a door in the eastern end of the building was battered down and a storming party rushed in.

Eight Chinamen were found within and dragged out to the
infuriated crowd. One was killed by dragging him through the
streets by a rope fastened to his neck, on the way to the place
of execution; three were hung on a wagon on Los Angeles
Street; four on the western gate of the Tomlinson corral, the
gate upon which Lachenais, the murderer of Bell, met his fate.
The crowd appeared maddened with the taste of blood, and
clamored for "more." It is stated that several other Chinamen,
not captured in the house where the murderers took refuge, fell
victims to the thirst for vengeance. At this hour it is impossible
to ascertain the exact number of casualties, but it is known
that fifteen Chinamen were hanged, three shot to death, and
that one of the wounded will die of his wounds. One Chinaman
was cut down, and his life saved when nearly extinct. Numbers
of Chinese fled the city, and took refuge in the country; several
gave themselves up at the county jail; others were captured
by small squads, and placed in jail for safety . . . with the cries
of hang! hang! hang! ringing in their ears.[7]

The New York Times reprinted from the San Francisco
Bulletin an account of the massacre which provides a
further dimension to the episode:

One of the most horrible tragedies that ever disgraced any
civilized community. . . . The denizens of Nigger Valley are
cosmopolitan, consist of the dregs of society, some of the
greatest desperadoes on the Pacific Coast. Murderers, horse-
thieves, highwaymen, burglars . . . make this their rendezvous.
In this place also the Chinese Congregate, monopolizing about
two-thirds of an entire block . . . The streets rattled with a
deafening din. . . . The entire block was surrounded by an
unbroken link of human devils, thirsting for revenge. Curses
and loud denunciations of the whole "heathen" crew arose on
all sides. . . . The yelling and cursing were frightful to hear.
. . . Trembling, moaning, wounded Chinese were hauled from

their hiding places; ropes quickly enriched their necks; they were dragged to the nearest improvised gallows. Three thus suffered in a cluster, to the end of a water spout. A large wagon close by had four victims hanging from its sides . . . Three others dangled from an awning . . . Five more were taken to the gateway and lynched . . . Hellish proceedings. . . . A little urchin, not over ten years old, was as active as anyone in doing the hanging. His childish voice sounded strange at that place, as he called aloud for more victims; a stranger and sadder sight still to see him lay his hands to the rope and help to haul them up. In the background a woman was looking on. . . . She loudly congratulated the lynchers on their diabolical work, and encouraged them to continue . . . Every nook, corner, chest, trunk, and drawer in Chinatown was carefully ransacked. Even the victims executed were robbed. The Chinese Doctor had his garments stripped from off his person while hanging; others had their pockets cut out with knives, which entered into and fearfully lacerated the flesh, the lynchers having neither time nor patience to rifle them in the usual way! . . . $6000 was extracted from a box in the Chinese store.[8]

The lead editorial in the same issue of the Los Angeles *Star* which contained the account of the massacre reflects the lack of remorse felt in the community over the violence perpetrated against the Chinese:

The *Chinese* Outrage
The horrible assassinations which were perpetrated in our city last night by the brutal, uncivilized barbarians that infest the country, is an indication of what the consequence would be were their race transmigrated in large numbers upon this coast. Upon all the earth there does not exist a people who value life so lightly, who practice so many horrors, or who are so unmerciful in their outrages. From their very mode of existence they have little regard for their own lives and none

whatever for the lives of others. The shooting of four of our citizens upon the streets yesterday, ere daylight had gone, and the frequency of their horrible acts of a similar nature, has now, at last, set our citizens to thinking as to the best mode of ridding ourselves of such a living curse. Little doubt exists but that such measures will be immediately taken as will entirely rid the city of their accursed presence. In this matter we should little heed the opinions of those abroad, who are not familiar with the Chinese nature and our circumstances. Have we not seen—have we not sadly realized? During the excitement last night several methods were proposed, among which was one, that a brief period of time be allowed for every Chinaman to leave the country. The most moderate course which could be pursued would be to withhold from them all business and all employment.

After all the above was written, last night, eighteen Chinamen were hanged and shot to death. The friends of the killed and wounded Americans were exasperated to such a degree that all attempts to quell the hanging and shooting were without avail, until the very horror of the scenes became sickening to the participators themselves. Comment is useless.[9]

One year later a number of the rioters were sent to San Quentin. But a little more than a year after that the California State Supreme Court summarily reversed the Los Angeles jury's verdict which had sent them to prison on the grounds that the indictment was "fatally defective in that it fails to allege that Chee Long Tong (one of the victims whose murder was seen by witnesses who were willing to testify) was murdered."[10]

The hostility of the Californians ultimately drove many Chinese laborers out of that state and into Oregon and the Northern Territories. Furthermore, the railroad building in these regions, the development of resources, and the growth of industry encouraged the Chinese to settle and work there.

There was general labor unrest in the country during the 1870's as a result of the economic depression which began with the Panic of 1873. Strikes marked by violence were the rule throughout the East. The West was not spared the problems of the depression years, especially the loss of jobs. Much of this suffering was laid at the door of the Chinese.

One of the earliest and most brutal among the many incidents of violence between the American natives and the Chinese immigrants took place at Rock Springs, in the Territory of Wyoming in 1885.[11] Whites had worked the mines at Rock Springs until a strike was called in 1875. The Union Pacific Railroad, owners of the mines, felt compelled to bring in about a hundred and fifty Chinese laborers to work the mines with the fifty whites who were not striking. In following years the number of Chinese and whites alike was increased. The proportion remained about one-third white and two-thirds Chinese.

Ten years later, during the summer of 1885, the general unrest caused by a new business decline in 1882 and the increasing anti-Chinese feeling which had been growing for years in the Far West began to surface. In the immediate background of the riot which took place at Rock Springs in September was resentment against the Union Pacific Coal Department for alleged mistreatment of workers. Smoldering race prejudice fanned into raging hatred by the refusal of the Chinese to join the strikes. There were 150 whites and 331 Chinese employed in the mines at this time. Many of the white miners were members of the Knights of Labor, a powerful union which among other things worked for the exclusion of Chinese laborers from the United States. Testimony in later investigations clearly indicated that the union supported and encouraged the events which led to the riot.[12]

It is said that mine bosses have favored the Chinamen to the detriment of white miners, and it needed only a spark to kindle the flames. This was furnished by a quarrel between a party of [Chinese] and whites in mine no. 6 over their right to work in a certain chamber. A fight ensued and the Chinamen were worsted, four of them being badly wounded, one of whom has since died. The white miners then came out, armed themselves with firearms, and notified . . . the men in the other three mines to come out in the afternoon. Meantime all was excitement in Chinatown. The flag was hoisted as a warning, and the Chinese working in different parts of the camp fled to their quarters. After dinner the saloons closed and no liquor has since been sold. The miners gathered on the front streets, about 100 of them armed with guns, revolvers, hatchets and knives, and proceeded toward Chinatown. Before reaching there they sent a committee of three to warn the Chinamen to leave in an hour. This they agreed to do, and started to pack up, but in about half an hour the white men became impatient and advanced upon the Chinese quarters, shouting and firing their guns into the air. Without offering resistance the Chinese fled with whatever they could snatch up. They fled to the hills about a mile east of the town, the miners firing at them as they fled. The miners then set fire to some of the houses, and soon eight or ten of the largest houses were in flames. Half choked with fire and smoke, numbers of Chinamen came rushing from the burning buildings, and with blankets and quilts over their heads to protect themselves from stray rifle shots, they followed their retreating brothers into the hills at the top of their speed.

A laundry in town was next visited and their inoffensive inmates shot dead. All the employees of the coal department of the railroad were ordered to leave town, which they did on the evening train. During the night all the Chinese houses in town, numbering fifty, were burned to the ground. A number of Chinamen who were hiding fled from the buildings. It is rumored that the Mormon miners in the camp are to be ordered out, but no action in that direction has yet been taken.

A glance over the battleground of Wednesday reveals the fact that many of the bullets fired at the fleeing Chinamen found their mark. Lying in the smoldering embers where Chinatown stood were found ten charred and shapeless trunks, sending up a noisome stench, while another, which had evidently been dragged from the ashes by boys, was found in the sage bush near by. A search resulted in the finding of the bodies of five more Chinamen, killed by rifle shots while fleeing from their pursuers. Some six or eight were found seriously wounded, and were cared for by railroad officers. The coroner's jury has rendered a verdict to the effect that men have come to their death at the hands of parties unknown.[13]

On that same afternoon word reached the governor that rioting was taking place at Rock Springs. An appeal for protection was made, but since there was no Territorial militia, Governor Warren of Wyoming Territory appealed to President Cleveland. Although the troops arrived after the savagery was committed and the damage done, the local press was outraged at the presence of troops:

Last Saturday morning our citizens were somewhat surprised to see a company of soldiers from Fort Steele get off a special train and go into camp near the railway at the west end of town. The troops are supposed to be here for the protection of property; but as not a threat or a movement has been made against the person or property of a single individual in town since the Chinese were driven out, the presence of the troops was entirely uncalled for. The impression is conveyed that the people in Rock Springs are a lawless, bloodthirsty set of people who can only be prevented from indiscriminate murder and arson by the presence of a body of armed troops. This is entirely false. The removal of the Chinese was all that was desired, and when they were driven from town the entire purpose of the outbreak was accomplished, and the life and property of other people were as safe here as in any other place . . .

If it is a disgrace for a few American miners, aggravated by a long course of injustice, *to kill a few Chinamen,* is it not a more damnable disgrace to see a rich and powerful corporation—created and sustained by American citizens—claiming and receiving the assistance of American soldiers to enforce the employment of leprous aliens to the exclusion of American workingmen? Why, even the soldiers themselves curse the duty which compels them to sustain the alien against the American, and no wonder every man in town is hot with indignation at the spectacle.[14]

Demonstrations and near riots took place in almost every town in Wyoming. The Chinese were warned to leave, strikes were carried out, and the cry of "The Chinese must go!" resounded from one end of the Territory to the other.

The Chinamen driven out of Rock Springs are gradually being picked up by trains going West and taken to Evanston, where 1000 Chinamen are living. These Chinese residents of Evanston are preparing to defend themselves, and purchase all the guns and ammunition in the market.[15]

While the company was in no mood to follow the dictates of the white miners and their union, it did alter its policy and no more Chinese workers were added to the payroll. By 1930 there were only a hundred and thirty Chinese in the entire state and none were working in the Union Pacific mines. The violence paid off.

Violence and the threat of violence against the Chinese disappeared only when Congress responded by excluding the yellow race through legislative fiat. In the twentieth century, when there was an upturn in Japanese immigration, anti-Japanese agitation crystallized into restrictive legislation. Much of present-day Asian contempt for this country has its origins in the violent treatment accorded the yellow race in our national past. No nonwhite race has escaped the American tradition.

NOTES

1. "Oriental Immigration," *Outlook*, Vol. LXXVII (1907), pp. 99–100.
2. Robert Louis Stevenson, *Across the Plains* (New York, 1892), p. 62.
3. The standard works on the anti-Chinese movement are Mary Roberts Coolidge, *Chinese Immigration* (New York, 1909); and Elmer C. Sandmyer, *The Anti-Chinese Movement in California* (Urbana, Illinois, 1939).
4. See Paul M. De Fella, "Lantern in the Western Sky," *Historical Society of Southern California Quarterly*, Vol. XLII (1960), pp. 57–88, 161–185; Chester P. Dorland, "Chinese Massacre at Los Angeles in 1871," *Historical Society of Southern California Annual*, Vol. III (1894), pp. 22–26; and William R. Locklear, "The Celestials and the Angels," *Historical Society of Southern California Quarterly*, Vol. XLII (1960), pp. 239–256.
5. Los Angeles *Star*, June 11, 1870.
6. See Locklear, *op. cit.*, p. 241.
7. Los Angeles *Star*, October 27, 1871.
8. *The New York Times*, October 27, 1871.
9. Los Angeles *Star*, October 27, 1871.
10. Quoted in De Fella, *op. cit.*, p. 184.

11. See Paul Crane and Alfred Larson, "The Chinese Massacre," *Annals of Wyoming,* Vol. XII (1940), pp. 47–55.
12. See U.S. House Report, 49th Cong., 1st sess., Vol. 7, Doc. No. 2044 (Washington, D.C., 1885–1886), p. 12.
13. *The New York Times,* September 5, 1885, p. 5.
14. Quoted in *The Chinese Massacre at Rock Springs, Wyoming Territory* (Boston, 1886).
15. *The New York Times,* September 5, 1885, p. 5.

8

FRONTIER AND
VIGILANTE JUSTICE

*". . . they tasselled the oaks
with the carcasses of the wicked."*

Violence in America west of the Mississippi during what
we so romantically recall as the "frontier years" was
marked by shootings and hangings. American literature
in the past and television in the present offer this violence
as a badge of entertainment and even nostalgia.

A certain amount of lawlessness and crime is almost
inevitable in the settlement of a new country, but the
amount which characterized the American western frontier
probably surpasses any measure of reasonableness.

In the occupation of the Trans-Mississippi West the frontier
was the major backwash of the great stream of civilization in
the jetsam of society congregated. The reckless and turbulent
characters of the nation, fleeing from the restrictions of orderly
communities, sought out an area where they would find an
environment in which they could carry on without interference
their careers of crime and plunder. Each area had its quota of
those who had gone west to escape jail or to make easy fortunes

from the work of others. Nearly every mining camp had its claim jumpers and thugs. Every stagecoach trail attracted highwaymen yearning to unload shipments of gold. The entire West was flooded with horse thieves and cattle rustlers.[1]

What one Eastern visitor, Frederick Law Olmsted, ascribed to Texas in particular was equally applicable to most of the West:

> In the rapid settlement of the country, many an adebturer crossed the border, spurred by love of liberty, forfeited at home, rather than drawn by a love of adventure or of rich soil. . . . probably a more reckless and vicious crew was seldom gathered than that which peopled some parts of Eastern Texas at the time of its first resistance to the Mexican government. "G.T.T." (gone to Texas) was the slang appendage . . . to every man's name who had disappeared before the discovery of some rascality. Did a man emigrate thither, everyone was on the watch for the discreditable reason to turn up. . . .
>
> If your life were of the slightest use to anyone, you might be sure he would take it. It was safe only as you were in constant readiness to defend it. Horses and wives were of as little account as umbrellas in more advanced states. Everybody appropriated everything that suited him, running his own risk of a penalty. Justice descended into the body of Judge Lynch, sleeping when he slept, and when he awoke hewing down right and left for exercise and pastime.[2]

But the violence of the criminal element which was inevitably drawn to the frontier society is a form of personal violence which is not our essential interest in this study of social violence. It is true, however, that not infrequently incidents of individual or personal violence develop into small-scale "wars" which amount to social violence. A good example of this is the frontier feud, almost always an outgrowth of a real or perceived personal wrong calling for direct and violent retaliation. Ruthless and savage feuds represented much of the violence which prevailed in the West.[3]

Wayne Gard, one of our leading historians of the American frontier, has described a number of feuds which turned into major episodes of social violence.[4] One of the most famous of these was the feud between the so-called Regulators and Moderators which came to be known as the Shelby County War.

The "war," which took place near the eastern edge of Texas, was characterized by land frauds, horse stealing, and home burnings, and was triggered by an incident in the fall of 1840. A fugitive ruffian, Charles W. Jackson, rode up to Joseph G. Goodbread, who was sitting on a hitching rack in Shelbyville, and pointed his rifle at Goodbread, with whom he had had a quarrel. The surprised Goodbread thought that the difficulty had been settled amicably, and he told Jackson that he certainly harbored no animosity toward him.

> "Besides," he pleaded, "I'm unarmed."
> "So much the better!" exclaimed Jackson, as he shot his victim through the heart.[5]

Jackson, together with some other frontiersmen, then organized an armed company called the Shelby Guards, popularly known as the Regulators. Ostensibly organized to suppress horse thieving and cattle rustling, this gang actually spent its time and energies inflicting terrorist vengeance, such as horsewhipping and murder, on its "enemies."

The Moderators were organized to oppose this high-handed assumption of authority. While they contended that they were out to uphold law and order, their first aim was to kill Jackson, the leader of the Regulators. This they quickly accomplished by ambushing him.

The terrorist activities carried on by these two bands as they roved about the country drove some settlers to abandon their farms and discouraged others from coming to the area. The local press observed that the area was "shunned as another Sodom."

Pitched battles between the two groups were fought in the summer of 1844, and at that point General Sam Houston, President of the Texas Republic, stepped in. Backed by a show of strength from a body of militiamen, he issued a proclamation dispersing both warring factions.

The violence which may have initially arisen between individual sheepmen and cattlemen frequently turned into range wars, and these clashes were certainly true forms of social violence. One noted chronicler, Emerson Hough, characterized the cattleman's low esteem for sheepmen: "The consensus of opinion was that no man engaged in walking sheep could be a decent citizen. He was a low-down, miserable being, whom it was correct to terrify or kill."[6]

But the typical conflicts between cattlemen and sheepmen were not personal or social feuds. They were expressions of economic rivalry between two groups competing for the limited grass and water available on the plains.

Cattlemen contended that the sheep destroyed the grass by nibbling it too closely and by trampling roots with their sharp hoofs. A "sheeped-off" range was thereby ruined as far as they were concerned. They complained about the odor left by the sheep, because this scent remained for hours afterward and neither the horses nor the cattle would graze or even drink the water.

The result was that bands of cattlemen, angered by the intrusion of the flocks on ranges they claimed (although they were in fact owned by the government), engaged in clubbing, shooting, dynamiting, poisoning, and burning the sheep, and stampeding them over cliffs. Sheep owners and herders were ordered to leave the ranges; some of them were killed.

There were numerous violent encounters between the sheepmen and cattlemen in the late nineteenth and early twentieth centuries. Eventually the cattlemen learned to take advantage of some of the positive factors contributed by sheep, and finally learned they could profit by raising some sheep along with their cattle.

Another form of violence along the frontier was that carried on among Texas cowmen in what has come to be known as the Fence-Cutter's War.[7] Before the invention of barbed wire, Texas had few fences of any kind. By the 1830's barbed wire became common in Texas. At first some stockmen ridiculed the "newfangled" fencing, but far-sighted ones understood the advantages of controlling their own pastures. They began buying land with good grass and water, and fencing it.

But not all cowmen had the vision or the money to buy

and fence ranches. Many of those with small herds continued to graze them on what was left of the open range,
most of it still owned by the state. As they saw fences
enclosing choice pastures along streams, they became
alarmed. Fencing made it harder for them to find enough
grass and, in dry spells, water for their herds.

A severe drought in 1883 brought things to a head. The
grass withered and became useless. The earth cracked.
Creeks dried up. Prairie fires added to the disaster.

The growing resistance of the landless cowmen to fencing
was encouraged by the Texas Greenback party, which
regarded barbed wire as a symbol of monopoly. The
fencers, it complained, were trying to turn the farmers
and small stockmen into serfs.

To these stockmen, barbed wire as an instrument of
the devil. They sent letters and telegrams to their representatives in the legislature and to the governor. Public
meetings were held. Finally, when no action resulted from
their pleas and complaints, many decided that the only
thing to do was to take action on their own. They would
cut the offending fences.

The desperate cattlemen formed small, secret bands, with
passwords and spies. All over the state, fences were being
destroyed by these saboteurs. As the drought became worse,
some of the cutters destroyed not only unlawful fences
but also those that enclosed land legitimately owned by
the fencers.

The situation grew so serious by the end of the year that
the governor called for legislation to severely punish fence
cutting as a felony, but at the same time to make the

building of illegal fences only a misdemeanor. Despite the disparity between the penalties for the two offenses, enforcement of these laws did bring about a gradual decrease in the fence troubles.

The frontier tradition of taking the law into one's own hands was hard to resist; and the Fence-Cutters' War was a well-intentioned effort to seek justice through group or social violence. In the end, however, fencing prevailed and the era of the open range was closed, making possible the settling of the Western plains.

Another example of a cattleman's "war" was the Johnson County Invasion, as it was called, which took place in Wyoming in 1892.[8] Again, the conflict was rooted in economic factors. It was between the big Wyoming cattlemen who came in early and without authority claimed most of the best land, and the small stockmen and farmers who arrived later and acquired free land under the Homestead Acts.

For several years prior to 1892, there were acts of violence on the part of so-called cattle barons against the small cattlemen on the pretext that the latter were guilty of cattle rustling. A number of the cattlemen were murdered, arousing the hatred of people in Johnson County against the barons. But none of them was ever punished for any of these murders.

In April, 1892, a group of these ranchmen brought into the county a special chartered train from Denver carrying two fifty-two heavily armed men and enough ammunition to wipe out the entire population of Wyoming. The pretext, again, was to eliminate cattle rustlers. In fact it was an attempt to settle the conflict that had been brewing for several years between the big cattlemen and the small cattlemen and farmers who had been pouring into the state and thereby challenging the monopoly of the big ranches.

The cattle barons' "invasion" began with an attack on a three-room cabin which contained two of the alleged rustlers they were after, Nick Ray and Nathan D. Champion.

"INVASION SONG"

I

Sad and dismal is the tale
  I now relate to you,
'Tis all about the cattlemen,
  Them and their murderous crew.
They started out on their man hunt,
  Precious blood to spill,
With a gang of hired assassins
  To murder at their will.

Refrain (repeated after each verse):
God bless poor Nate and Nick
  Who gave their precious lives
To save the town of Buffalo,
  Its brave men and their wives.
If it hadn't been for Nate and Nick
  What would we have come to?
We would all have been murdered by
  Frank Canton and his crew.

II

Poor Nate Champion is no more,
  He lost his precious life,
He lies down in the valley
  Freed from all care and strife.
He tried to run the gantlet
  When they burned his home
And Nick was lying lifeless,
  Lips wet with bloody foam.

III

The run was made; his doom was sealed,
  A fact you all know well.
They left his lifeless body there
  On the slope, above the dell.
No kindred near to care for him,
  To grasp his nerveless hand;
A braver man was never faced
  By Canton's bloody band.

IV

The very next name upon the list
  Was that of brave Jack Flagg.
Frank Canton must have surely thought
  That he would "fill his bag."
Jack and his stepson came in view
  A-riding round the curve;
"Throw up your hands! By God they're off!"
  Frank Canton lost his nerve.

V

"Red" Angus next, the "Canny Scot,"
  Was marked for Canton's lead;

But Angus, warned by bold Jack Flagg
  For aid and succor, sped.
The countryside now swarmed to life,
  The settlers armed in haste;
Soon Red had hundreds at his back
  Who Canton's minions faced.

VI

To Crazy Woman's winding bank
  The cowed invaders fled.
With K.C., blazing in their rear,
  And Ray and Champion dead.
Here, held at bay the cravens halt
  Till soldiers come to aid;
And now secure in jail they rest,
  The debt of blood, unpaid.[9]

What had happened was that three hundred and twenty homesteaders and townsmen routed the invaders and held them at bay until federal troops entered the scene and placed the invading group of forty-six men under arrest. They gave up forty-three rifles, forty-one pistols, forty-six horses, and about five hundred rounds of ammunition. The local sheriff asked the governor to turn over the prisoners for local civilian trial, but the Governor refused on the grounds that they might become objects of violence in Johnson County. In fact the men responsible for the murders of Champion and Ray, together with the members of the armed force engaged by the big cattlemen, all managed to get off without any punishment.

The Johnson County Invasion was the last of the serious range wars; those Westerners who continued to take justice into their own hands were mainly citizens who banded together as vigilantes.

A number of historians rationalize the committees of vigilance as a necessity, because there was no other effective action against crime in the frontier environment.[10] They contend that such groups and their activities had a large hand in making the frontier safe for settlement and in clearing the way for statutory law. But when the historical niceties are stripped away, the identifying character of this movement is group action in place of established justice, with the result that vigilantism permitted if not encouraged both collective and personal violence.

The raw brutality of vigilante "justice" in a frontier setting is graphically as well as philosophically described in this poignant excerpt from a work by Clarence King, a noted scientist in mid-eighteenth-century America:

> For a few years the solemn pines looked down on a mad carnival of godless license, a pandemonium in whose picturesque delirium human character crumbled and vanished like dead leaves.
>
> It was stirring and gay, but Melpomene's pathetic face was always under that laughing mask of comedy.
>
> This is the unpromising origin of our Sierra Civilization. It may be instructive to note some early steps of improvement; a protest, first silent, then loud, which went up against disorder and crime; and later, the inauguration of justice, in form if not reality.
>
> There occurs to me an incident illustrating these first essays in civil law; it is vouched for by my friend, an unwilling actor in the affair.
>
> Exactly why horse stealing should have been so early recognized as a heinous sin it is not easy to discover; however that

might be, murderers continued to notch the number of their victims on neatly kept hilts of pistols or knives, in comparative security, long after the horse thief began to meet his hempen fate.

Early in the fifties, on a still, hot summer's afternoon, a certain man, in a camp in the northern mines which shall be nameless, having tracked his two donkeys and one horse a half-mile, and discovering that a man's track with spur-marks followed them, came back to town and told "the boys," who loitered about a popular saloon, that in his opinion some Mexican had stole the animals.

Such news as this naturally demanded drinks all round.

"Do you know, gentlemen," said one who assumed leadership, "that just naturally to shoot these Greasers ain't the best way. Give 'em a fair jury trial, and rope 'em up with all the majesty of the law. That's the cure."

Such words of moderation were well received, and they drank again to "here's hoping we ketch that Greaser." As they loafed back to the veranda a Mexican walked over the hill brow, jingling his spurs pleasantly in accord with a whistled waltz.

The advocate for law said in an undertone, "That's the cuss."

A rush, a struggle, and the Mexican, bound hand and foot, lay on his back in the bar-room. The camp turned out to a man.

Happily such cries as "string him up!" "Burn the dog-goned lubricator!" and other equally pleasant phrases fell unheeded upon his Spanish ear.

A jury, upon which they forced my friend, was quickly gathered in the street, and despite refusals to serve, the crowd hurried them in behind the bar.

A brief statement of the case was made by the *ci devant* advocate, and they shoved the jury into a commodious poker room, where were seats grouped about neat, green tables. The noise outside in the bar-room by and by died away into complete silence, but from afar down the canon came confused sounds as of disorderly cheering.

They came nearer, and again the light-hearted noise of human laughter mingled with clinking glasses around the bar.

A low knock at the jury door; the lock burst in, and a dozen smiling fellows asked the verdict.

A foreman promptly answered *"Not guilty."*

With volleyed oaths, and ominous laying of hands on pistol hilts, the boys slammed the door with, "You'll have to do better than that!"

In half an hour the advocate gently opened the door again. "Your opinion, gentlemen?"

"Guilty!"

"Correct! You can come out. We hung him an hour ago."

The jury took their next; and when, after a few minutes, the pleasant village returned to its former tranquility, it was "allowed" at more than one saloon that "Mexicans'll know enough to let white men's stock alone after this." One and another exchanged the belief that this sort of thing was more sensible than "nipping 'em on sight."

When, before sunset, the bar-keeper concluded to sweep some dust out of his poker-room back-door, he felt a momentary surprise at finding the missing horse dozing under the shadow of an oak, and the two lost donkeys serenely masticating playing-cards, of which many bushels lay in a dusty pile.

He was reminded then that the animals had been there all day.

During three or four years the battle between good and bad became more and more determined, until all positive characters arrayed themselves either for or against public order.

At length, on a sudden, the party for right organized those august mobs, the Vigilance Committees, and quickly began to festoon their more depraved fellowmen from tree to tree. Rogues of sufficient shrewdness got themselves enrolled in the vigilance ranks, and were soon unable to tell themselves from the most virtuous. Those quiet oaks, whose hundreds of sunny years had been spent in lengthening out glorious branches, now found themselves playing the part of public gibbet.

Let it be distinctly understood that I am not passing criticism on the San Francisco organization, which I have never investigated, but on "Committees" in the mountain towns, with whose performance I am familiar.

The Vigilantes quickly put out of existence a majority of the worst desperadoes, and, by their swift, merciless action, struck such terror to the rest, that ever after, the right has mainly controlled affairs.

This was, *perhaps,* well. With characteristic promptness they laid down their power, and gave California over to the constituted authorities. This was magnificent. They deserve the commendation due success. They have, however, such a frank, honest way of singing their praise, such eternal, undisguised and virtuous self-laudation over the whole matter, that no one else need interrupt them with fainter notes.

Although this generation has written its indorsement in full upon the transaction, it may be doubted if history (how long is it before dispassionate candor speaks?) will trace an altogether favorable verdict upon her pages. Possibly, to fulfil the golden round of duty, it is needful to do right in the right way, and success may not be proven the eternal test of merit.

That the Vigilance Committees grasped the moral power is undeniable; that they used it for the public salvation is equally true; but the best advocates are far from showing that with skill and moderation they might not have thrown their weight into the scale *with* law, and conquered, by means of legislature, judge, and jury, a peace wholly free from the stain of lawless blood.

An impartial future may possibly grant the plenary inspiration of Vigilance Committees. Perhaps that better choice was in truth denied them; it may be the hour demanded a sudden blow of self-defence. Whether better or best, the act has not left unmixed blessings, although it now seems as if the lawlessness, which even till these later years (1871) has from time to time manifested itself, is gradually and surely dying out. Yet to-day, as I write, State troops are encamped at Amador, to suppress a spirit which has taken law in its own hand.[11]

The work of the vigilante committees, then, was held up as a form of social action against bad men. Conditions in the West sharpened conflict and favored resort to violence as the one way to accomplish things. Men made their own law on the spot, caught horse thieves and other outlaws, and hanged them to the nearest cottonwood. As Bancroft, a historian, puts it, they "tasselled the oaks with the carcasses of the wicked."[12]

Today's beyond-the-law tactics have their roots in the frontier vigilantism which too many Americans regard as a glorified part of the pioneer heritage. The work of the present-day Ku Klux Klan should, however, serve as a harsh reminder of the havoc wrought by the violent tradition of vigilante activity.

NOTES

1. William C. Holden, "Law and Lawlessness on the Texas Frontier," *Southwestern Historical Quarterly*, Vol. XLIV (1940), p. 188. For the most recent and comprehensive treatment of all aspects of vigilantism, see Richard M. Brown, "The American Vigilante Tradition," *Violence in America: Historical and Comparative Perspectives*, A Report Submitted to the National Commission on the Causes and Prevention of Violence (Bantam Book Edition, New York, 1969), Chapter 5.
2. Frederick Law Olmsted, *Journey Through Texas* (New York, 1857), p. 118.
3. Violent personal feuds were carried on rather widely into the twentieth century. See Hartley Davis and Clifford Smyth, "The Land of the Feuds," *Munsey's Magazine*, Vol. XXX (1903), pp. 161–172. Subtitled "The Terrible Story of the 7 Great Kentucky Feuds," this account described Kentucky as the worst among the four states which meet in the heart of the Appalachian Mountains: "A savage, primeval country, where have developed those fierce and terrible family wars, the American feuds, beside which the Italian vendetta is a childish thing, almost humane in comparison . . . among these people the lust for human blood has become a malignant disease" (p. 162). Some two hundred and fifty murders were committed during the period of these feuds.

4. This account is largely drawn from Wayne Gard's *Frontier Justice* (Norman, Oklahoma, 1949). This is the most comprehensive and most documented study of frontier violence presently available, and deserves the attention of any reader who seeks further information on the subject.

5. Quoted in *ibid.*, p. 22.

6. Emerson Hough, *The Story of the Cowboy* (New York, 1897).

7. See R. D. Holt, "The Introduction of Barbed Wire Into Texas and the Fence-Cutting War," *West Texas Historical Association Year Book*, Vol. VI (1930), pp. 65–79.

8. See Gard, *op. cit.*, Chapter 7.

9. Levette J. Davidson, "A Ballad of the Wyoming Rustler War," *Western Folklore*, Vol. VI (1947).

10. Wayne Gard takes this position in his work, *Frontier Justice*. For a persuasive refutation of this position, and a highly readable one, see John W. Caughey, *Their Majesties the Mob* (Chicago, 1960).

11. Clarence King, *Mountaineering in the Sierra Nevada* (Boston, 1871), 283–287.

12. Hubert H. Bancroft, *Popular Tribunals*, 2 vols. (San Francisco, 1887; New York, 1967). Bancroft wrote a thirty-nine-volume history of the Pacific states of North America, devoting these two volumes alone to what he called the "popular tribunals."

9

LABOR STRUGGLES

". . . they will be mowed down like grass before a scythe."

The story of labor violence encompasses social, political, and of course economic factors, all combined to a degree unmatched in the other episodes presented in this work. Indeed labor's struggle for recognition as well as for material gains is perhaps the classic example of the use of violence to achieve social change in America.

It was the depression of the 1870's, triggered by the Panic of 1873, which ushered in the first major period of violence in American labor history and one of the most violent decades in the nation. This was, after all, the same decade which witnessed the terror of the Ku Klux Klan in the South, the lawlessness of the Western frontier, the Chinese massacres and vigilante committees of the Far West, the Anti-Catholic riots in Eastern cities, violence in the mining regions, and finally labor violence throughout the country.

The great railroad strikes which made 1877 the year of the "great upheaval" were the expression of a deep and accumulated discontent—always a backdrop to social violence.[1] Labor outbreaks had been common enough in the country before this time, but they were always confined to the individual areas of local companies. This was the first nationwide uprising of the workers, one so vast and so violent that it was crushed only after a good deal of blood was spilled.

On the face of it, the strikes were a protest against wage cuts. They had, however, a deeper origin in the depression brought about by the 1873 economic panic.[2] This crash drove workers in many of the big cities to press for government intervention and larger programs of public works to help the increasing number of unemployed. Demonstrations and marches took place in New York, Chicago, Cincinnati, and Philadelphia. In many of these affairs workers were the victims of strong government suppression supported especially by the local newspapers. The Tompkins Square Riot in New York City on January 13, 1874, was typical. Denied a permit to hold a mass meeting in front of city hall, the workers' committee agreed to conduct a rally of protest at Union Square. At the last minute the committee canceled the Union Square meeting and announced a "mass indignation meeting" in Tompkins Square Park the next morning. At the request of the police department, the department of parks canceled the permit to meet in the park. Without knowing about the police decision, thousands of men, women, and children jammed the park.

Police Commissioner Abram Duryee, surrounded by detectives and accompanied by a number of patrolmen with drawn sticks, marched into the center of the crowd and ordered the park and streets nearby emptied of the thousands of people in them.[3] A New York *Sun* reporter described what followed:

> The rapidly moving crowd did not look behind. They simply yelled and moved as fast as their legs would carry them. Captain Speight's men were close at their heels, their horses galloping full speed on the sidewalks. Men tumbled over each other . . . into the gutter or clambered up high steps to get out of the way of the chargers. The horsemen beat the air with their batons and many persons were laid low. . . .[4]

Samuel Gompers, who avoided a beating on the head "by jumping into a cellarway," remembered the police action as "an orgy of brutality." The fighting continued for a few more hours. Gompers insisted that the police were beating any "group of poorly dressed persons standing or moving together." When large crowds gathered around the Fifth Street Police Station and called for the release of imprisoned workers, the police charged them again and again. A reporter described the police as "seized with a fit of St. Vitus dance. It was only a question of luck who was clubbed and who was not."[5] A prominent clergyman supported the police for teaching the workers that "if they lift their hands against law, order, and good government, they will be mowed down like grass before a scythe."[6]

One other outbreak of violence which marked the years before the climactic railroad strikes of 1877 was the violence in the anthracite coal fields of eastern Pennsylvania. The workers in this industry had formed a union of their own and reached an agreement with the Anthracite

Trade Board. In December, 1874, the operators independently cut wages below the agreed minimum. The miners walked out of the pits, and in what became known as "the long strike," they tried to force the operators to restore the cuts. Many of the strikers could not endure the sustained unemployment, which meant a lack of food and sometimes even shelter, and they returned to the pits. But close to open warfare developed between the remaining strikers and the coal-and-iron police sent into the area by the operators to protect strikebreakers.

Into this situation there entered another group whose exact role in the long strike is still impossible to determine. At the time sensational reports appeared in the press on the operations of a secret organization among the miners, the Ancient Order of Hibernians, more popularly known as the Molly Maguires.[7] Molly Maguire was a legendary Irish revolutionary who fought against British control of Ireland. This group was charged with terrorizing the coal fields and preventing those miners who wished to work from doing so. Sabotage and destruction of property, outright murder and assassination, were all charged against its members. It was revealed many years later, in 1947, that the operators themselves had instigated some of these attacks on the mines in order to provide an excuse for moving in, not only to crush the Molly Maguires but also all union organizations.[8]

By 1877 the depression had reached its lowest point. The railroads, which had been cutting wages steadily, prepared for another reduction so that they could reduce freight rates. By the middle of July all the major lines followed the lead of the Pennsylvania Railroad, which had made a ten-percent cut on June 1. With thousands of jobless men seeking employment, the railroad officials were confident that the workers would be afraid to walk out, regardless of their anger at the move.

However, strikes broke out almost immediately to protest the wage cuts, the first one being against the Baltimore & Ohio. It was at Martinsburg, in West Virginia, that the first violence occurred. The local state militia was sent into the town by the governor at the request of the railroad. But the militia would not fire or otherwise use force on the strikers, who took possession of the railroad cars and prevented them from being moved. Under the circumstances, the governor turned to the federal government for assistance.

Wheeling, W. Va., July 18th.

To His Excellency R. B. Hayes, President of the United States:
Owing to unlawful combinations and domestic violence now existing at Martinsburg and other points along the line of the Baltimore & Ohio Railroad, it is impossible with any force at my command to execute the laws of the State. I therefore call upon your Excellency for the assistance of the United States military to protect the law-abiding people of the State against domestic violence, and to maintain the supremacy of law. . . .[9]

Federal military intervention in a labor dispute was not unprecedented.[10] President Andrew Jackson, by request of the Maryland legislature, had sent federal troops to quell a labor riot among construction workers on the Chesapeake and Ohio Canal forty-three years before. Furthermore, the Reconstruction period had accustomed Americans to the maintenance of peace by federal troops on the application of a state governor. President Hayes sent in two hundred troops and order was restored in Martinsburg. But the strike was just beginning.

It was in Baltimore that violence now broke out. Early in the nineteenth century Baltimore had taken Boston's place as the "most mobbish" town in the country. The depression had hit hard at all Baltimore's wage earners. A large number of canmakers, garmentworkers and box-makers were on strike in July, 1877. The striking rail-roaders were quiet at the outset; the violent ones had given vent to their energies in Martinsburg, Cumberland, and other points along the line.

On the evening of July 17 the *Evening Bulletin* warned "those contemplating violence" to remember that "they are not in Martinsburg . . . [Baltimore] cannot afford to have any rioting, and all acts leading to it must be promptly repressed."[11]

The strikers nevertheless stopped all trains, refused to allow them to move, and began to seize railroad property. When the militia, called out by the governor, marched from the armory to the railway station, a gathering mob of workers and their sympathizers attacked them with stones and clubs. Full-scale violence had set in. The troops opened fire and broke for the station, but the rioters had had a taste of blood. They kept up the assault and set fire to the station. When police and firemen arrived, the mob tried to prevent them from putting out the blaze, but finally they gave way. Violence went on through a wild and riotous night, and only the arrival of federal troops the next morning brought any return of order.

A number of the soldiers were severely wounded by the mob. Among the rioters nine were killed, two mortally wounded, and a number wounded by the fire of the troops. Two more rioters were shot by the police in the fight at the lower end of the depot. When the soldiers did fire directly on the mob, they did so in deadly earnest, as the vast preponderance of the dead over the wounded testifies. Almost every man shot was hit in either the chest or head, and nearly all the wounds were fatal.[12]

In the meantime Pittsburgh was having a riot bloodier than any the country had experienced since the Civil War draft riots in New York City. This was the most violent of the railroad clashes. The men on the Pennsylvania Railroad had accepted the wage cut of June 1, but there were other complaints. The company had broken faith with them on several of its lines. In 1873, for example, the brakemen's pay on one line had been cut from $1.58 to 85¢ per day of fifteen to eighteen hours. Noting that their wages were already low, the company had agreed that the ten-percent cut would not apply to them. Yet on July 6 posters appeared lowering their pay to 75¢ a day retroactive to June 1.

On July 19, 1877, the workers at Pittsburgh, goaded by the company's attitude and infected by the reports from the Baltimore & Ohio, left their trains without prearrangement and took over the switches. Soon they numbered over five hundred. By midnight about fourteen hundred men had gathered in the two yards of the Pennsylvania Railroad, and fifteen hundred cars were standing on the sidings.

Unable to cope with the outbreak, the company called on the city and county authorities for protection. The

sheriff of Allegheny County came on the scene in response
to the request, but the men refused to obey his order to
disperse. At this point the sheriff decided to call upon the
military.

> Pittsburgh, Pa., July 19th.
> To Hon. John F. Hartranft, Governor of Pennsylvania, Harris-
> burg, Pa.:
> Sir: A tumult, riot, and mob exist on the Pennsylvania Railroad
> at East Liberty and in the Twelfth Ward of Pittsburgh. Large
> assemblages of people are upon the railroad, and the movement
> of freight trains either east or west is prevented by intimidation
> and violence, molesting and obstructing the engineers and other
> employees of the railroad company in the discharge of their
> duties. As the sheriff of the county, I have endeavored to
> suppress the riot, but have not the adequate means at my
> command to do so, and I therefore request you to exercise your
> authority in calling out the military to suppress the same.
> R. C. Fide, Sheriff of Allegheny[13]

The governor promptly ordered out the Sixth Division
of the militia at Pittsburgh. But the troops merely looked
on while the workmen met all freight trains entering the
yards and persuaded the crews to join the strike. Much of
the local population, including many businessmen who
felt they were discriminated against in freight rates, was
sympathetic to the strikers. More than nine hundred loaded
cars stood idle the next day on the track between the Union
Depot and East Liberty.

Once Governor Hartranft saw that the local militia could
not be depended upon to move against the strikers, he called
for troops from Philadelphia, apparently depending on
the old rivalry between the two cities. The Pennsylvania

Railroad made all arrangements for transporting the militia from Philadelphia, and ammunition was shipped from the state arsenal at Harrisburg. The detachment of one thousand troops, including a battery of artillery, came into the Union Depot at noon on Saturday, July 21. The trains carrying them bore marks of heavy stoning by mobs along the way. As they rode into the yard, the Philadelphia soldiers saw more than two thousand cars and locomotives lying idle around them. Cars which had contained perishable items were empty, but many cars still held all the necessities and most of the luxuries of nineteenth-century civilization.[14]

At about half past three the troops began to march from Liberty Street to Twenty-eighth Street to disperse the strikers. They were under strict orders not to shoot except in self-defense. Thousands of men, women, and children had gathered about the troops, most of them taunting the soldiers with shouts of "Shoot!" "Shoot, you sons of bitches, why don't you shoot!" Some stones were thrown and then shots were fired by strikers from behind the coal cars. At this point the mob began heaving rocks, and a number of the soldiers were seriously wounded. The troops began to fire. For about ten minutes they fired heavily and aimlessly in all directions. An estimated twenty people were killed during this ten-minute melee, none of them soldiers.[15] As soon as the crowd started retreating, a "Cease fire!" command was called out, and within minutes there was silence in the almost empty area.

News of the slaughter at Twenty-eighth Street spread through the city and enraged the population.

By eight o'clock in the evening the mobs were moving about the city in various directions, sacking stores to secure arms, breaking into the armories of the military companies, and preparing themselves to execute threats freely expressed of massacring the entire Philadelphia command. The city was at this time virtually in the hands of an utterly irresponsible mob, composed only in small part, however, of railroad hands, but more of laborers and iron workers, coal miners, stevedores, and others who were in full sympathy with the strikers. A large mob visited Johnson's gun factory on Smithfield Street, about seven o'clock in the evening, and armed themselves. Another still larger crowd demolished Brown's establishment on Wood Street, which they completely gutted, and then marched down Fifth Avenue, with drums beating and flags flying; about three thousand in number.[16]

The troops retreated to the roundhouse and took possession of the machine shops. The angry mobs returned to the attack with arms seized from nearby gunshops and laid siege to the troops. As night fell, freight cars were set afire and pushed into the roundhouse until it, too, was blazing. Surrounded by flames and nearly suffocated, the troops fought their way out through the crowd, killing twenty more and losing a handful of their own men, until they were able to escape to Sharpsburg across the Allegheny River.

The field was now clear for what had become a mob of thousands. Railway tracks were torn up, freight and passenger cars broken up, and what could not otherwise be destroyed was set afire. Some two thousand cars, the machine shops, a grain elevator, and two roundhouses with a hundred and twenty-five locomotives went up in flames.

The Union Depot itself was burned down. As the rioting continued unchecked, men and women broke into liquor stores and began to pillage. They looted furniture, clothing, and provisions of every kind.

> While hundreds were engaged in firing the cars and making certain of the destruction of the valuable buildings at the outer depot, thousands of men, women, and children engaged in pillaging the cars. Men armed with heavy sledges would break open the cars, and then the contents would be thrown out and carried off by those bent on profiting by the reign of terror. The street was almost completely blockaded by persons laboring to carry off the plunder they had gathered together. In hundreds of instances wagons were pressed into service to enable the thieves to get away with their goods. . . .[17]

The total loss to the Pennsylvania Railroad was over five million dollars. For two miles along the railroad there was wreckage and smoldering ruin.

Other cities in Pennsylvania were affected by the strikes —Altoona, Easton, Harrisburg, Reading, Johnstown, Bethlehem, Philadelphia. Freight was tied up on the entire line. State and federal troops finally moved into the area in great numbers, with more than ten thousand troops concentrated along the sixty miles of railroad between Pittsburgh and Blairsville. Governor Hartranft opened the divisions in succession, starting west from Harrisburg. In every city the strike leaders were arrested and held without bail. On July 28 the governor entered Pittsburgh commanding four troop trains, with a Gatling gun mounted on a gondola car in front of the first locomotive. By nightfall three thousand troops had arrived in the city. In spite of stubborn opposition, the freight blockade was slowly broken. The Pennsylvania Railroad issued a notice that beginning Monday, July 30, all its lines would be open for passengers and freight.

Headlines and editorials declared that communism was at the bottom of the strike and responsible for its violence throughout the country. *The New York Times* declared that the only logic the strikers knew was the logic of force; it was futile to show mercy to the "ignorant rabble with hungry mouths." To the New York *Herald* the mob "is a wild beast and needs to be shot down." The New York *Sun* suggested a diet of lead for the strikers, while *The Nation* called for federal sharpshooters.[18]

The Pittsburgh debacle triggered a chain reaction which "acted on the nation like a hot coal in a barrel of fire-crackers."[19] From coast to coast the strike spread and blood spilled, but the strikers knew they were beaten once the federal government backed the railroads. As they had done in Pennsylvania, federal troops snuffed out the rioting in city after city in other states. By the end of July the trains were generally running again and the strikes were over.

The outbreaks of violence and mob action had demanded vigorous enforcement of law and order, but in the suppression of the strikes, the original grievances of the railway workers were completely overlooked. The disorder and rioting of July, 1877, showed labor that uncontrolled mob action largely invited suppression by state or federal troops rather than remedial action by industrial management or even sympathy from the public in response to the grievances which provoked strike action. However, even when labor began to develop its own organization and leadership, government and management still failed to meet labor's needs and demands within the framework of peaceful negotiations, so that violence continued to mark the labor-capital struggle until recent years.

Less than a decade after the violence of the railroad strikes, Chicago became the scene of another bloody episode, the Haymarket Riot. On the night of May 4, 1886, a peaceful meeting of three thousand workers was being held in Haymarket Square to protest the shooting of strikers by the police in the course of the McCormick Reaper Strike then being conducted in Chicago. Even the mayor attended. As the meeting began to disperse, someone threw a dynamite bomb into the front line of advancing policemen, who were demanding that the participants break up and leave the rally. Seven of them were fatally injured. The police then fired into the crowd and there were answering shots from the workers. In addition to some sixty-seven injured policemen, four workers were killed and fifty more injured.

Although the identity of the bomb thrower was never established, eight known anarchist leaders were arrested and tried for the deed, and found guilty. Four were executed for murder and one committed suicide in jail. There was a general feeling that the eight anarchists were convicted on the basis of their beliefs rather than on any evidence of their participation in the crime, a feeling which persists to this day.[20] Two of the defendants had their death sentences changed to life imprisonment by the Illinois governor. Six years later, another governor, John Peter

Altgeld, pardoned the imprisoned anarchists. He accompanied his pardon with a statement which cost him his political life and career. He declared that the betrayal of democracy and justice in the Haymarket trial was a greater menace to America than anything the defendants had ever thought or done.

One of the major episodes of labor violence in American history was the strike at the Carnegie Steel Company plant in Homestead, Pennsylvania.[21] The contestants in the battle were the company, forerunner of the United States Steel Corporation, and the Homestead Lodges of the Amalgamated Association of Iron and Steel Workers. The newly organized Carnegie Steel Company controlled almost the entire steel market in the country; it owned and operated twelve steel and coke works in the vicinity of Pittsburgh, and employed thirteen thousand men. The Amalgamated Association of Iron and Steel Workers had twenty-five thousand members, all skilled men, and was one of the most powerful trade unions in the history of the American labor movement.

The borough of Homestead, scene of the struggle, is on the left bank of the Monongahela River, seven miles east of Pittsburgh. It was then a dependent community around the nucleus of steel works, where almost a third of its ten to twelve thousand inhabitants were employed.

Ever since 1889, when the workers had won a strike by turning back one hundred deputies who had been sent from Pittsburgh to guard the steel works and permit the introduction of "blacksheep," or nonunion, men, the relations between the company and its employees had been unfriendly. The two parties had been operating on a sliding-scale wage agreement which was to expire on June 30, 1892.

Throughout these three years of the contract the company, a dominating power with feeble enough rivals, chafed under the necessity of dealing with the Amalgamated Association and dividing its profits with the men. Trouble was expected as the time approached for drawing up a new agreement. When Henry Clay Frick, known as the Coke King in the Connellsville district, fifty miles south of Pittsburgh, was given the managing authority of the company, the workers realized they would have to fight for the preservation of their union against the avowed and ruthless antiunion policy of the man who had already crushed several strikes by means of the Coal and Iron Police, the Pinkerton Detective Agency, and the state militia.

Negotiations for a new agreement opened in February, 1892, when a committee from the Amalgamated presented a scale to J. A. Potter, superintendent of the Homestead mill. Potter in turn handed the committee a scale from the company, providing for a reduction in wages and calling for a change in the termination date of the contract. The committee asked why a reduction was demanded, but received no explanation.

The men haggled with the company for the next three months, without coming to an agreement. On May 30 the company issued an ultimatum that the men would have to accept its scale before June 24. After that date the men would be dealt with individually.

Meanwhile preparations were being made at the Homestead works. A solid board fence was erected around the mill property. This fence was topped with barbed wire and was perforated at intervals for what appeared to be rifles, although Frick later contended that the holes were meant for observation. In the mill yards stood platforms equipped with searchlights. The workmen dubbed the mill Fort Frick.

At the request of the workers Frick met a committee from the Amalgamated in the company office at Pittsburgh for a final conference on June 23, the day before the execution of the ultimatum. No agreement was reached.

The workers were in the meantime angered by the obvious aggressiveness of the company and by the fortification thrown around the works even before negotiations ended. They hanged Frick in effigy on the mill property and turned the hose on men sent by the company to cut down the effigy. Using this incident as a reason, the company began to shut down the works on June 28, two days before the agreement with the Amalgamated was to end. By the morning of June 30 the entire work force was locked out.

The workers held a mass meeting at which the mechanics and unskilled laborers, who numbered nearly three thousand and who were not members of the union, determined nevertheless to stand with the eight hundred skilled union men against the company. To organize and direct the activities of the men, an advisory committee was formed, and the leadership was given to Hugh O'Donnell. The advisory committee soon had full control of the town. A strict guard was kept day and night around the steel works, and all approaches to both town and mill were watched; no one could enter without the consent of the committee. The men assigned to the different posts reported regularly to the headquarters, and a system of signaling was arranged, including the use of rockets at night, so that one thousand men could be deployed to any spot within five minutes. In addition to this, the committee communicated with Pittsburgh, Philadelphia, and other large cities to learn of any movement of blacksheep intended for Homestead.

On July 1, when Superintendent Potter and several foremen attempted to enter the mill, they were stopped at the gates by the locked-out men and induced to turn back. The workers were determined to prevent all preparations for the introduction of scabs; their attitude was that their labor had built up the industry, and they were entitled to the jobs. The company then notified the sheriff of Allegheny County, William H. McCleary, that one hundred deputies would be needed to protect the company property. McCleary went to Homestead to confer with the advisory committee of the workers. After some discussion the committee agreed that he would be allowed to come with fifty deputies to take possession of the mill.

Failing to get together a posse comitatus because the citizens refused to answer his summons to serve against the Homestead workers, McCleary was compelled to send his office force of twelve deputies; he himself did not accompany them. The deputies were met at the Homestead station by a crowd of two thousand men who permitted them to see that the mill property was intact and then informed them they would not be admitted into the steel works merely to provide entry for blacksheep. To the deputies the crowd seemed threatening and tense. A test of strength was expected shortly. Matters were further aggravated by newpaper reports that Potter and twenty of his foremen were searching in large cities for the two hundred and sixty skilled workers they needed to start the mill. As a result, the deputies were escorted to the river, put on a tugboat, and shipped back to Pittsburgh.

Frick figured that if he could get a force of armed Pinkerton detectives behind the fortifications at Homestead, it would be easy to fight off the workers and introduce the necessary scabs. As early as June 20, even before the negotiations with the Amalgamated were at an end, he had contacted Robert A. Pinkerton of New York, who had supplied him with two hundred detectives during a similar situation in the Connellsville coke region.

A letter from Frick on June 25 gave detailed instructions to the Pinkerton agency. Three hundred Pinkertons were to gather at Ashtabula, Ohio, on the morning of July 5 and were to proceed by rail to Youngstown. From there they were to be transported at night by boat up the river to Homestead. Since it might prove illegal to bring an armed force into the state, the rifles, pistols, batons, and ammunition were to be shipped separately in care of the Union Supply Company. The detectives were to be armed after they were within the boundaries of Pennsylvania. Frick agreed to pay five dollars a day for each man. In the meantime two barges were fitted up for the Pinkertons, one with bunks to serve as a dormitory, the other with tables to be used as a large refectory; and two steamboats were engaged to tow the barges.

According to plans, the Pinkerton train was met on

July 5 at Davis Island Dam, five or six miles below Pittsburgh; and while the barges proceeded silently up the river, the detectives armed themselves with Winchester rifles and put on the blue Pinkerton uniforms. But the detectives were sighted at four o'clock in the morning by a patrol about one mile below Homestead; soon whistles sounded a general alarm throughout the town, and a crowd of men, women, and children lined the river bank.

The barges pulled up to the company beach, where the wire-topped fence had been brought down to the low-water mark so as to cut off all access by land; and when the crowd on shore saw that the Pinkertons intended to land, it tore a gap in the fence and trespassed on the mill property for the first time. The workers warned the detectives to go back. A gangplank was shoved out and several Pinkertons started down it. Someone fired a shot. While it was never established who fired that first shot, it was clear that the Pinkertons then fired a volley into the crowd and brought down several workers. The women and children ran out of range of the rifles to watch the battle, while the men barricaded themselves behind ramparts of steel, pig iron, and scrap iron, and opened fire. The Pinkertons retreated into the shelter of their barges. The steamboats which had towed the barges took on board two or three wounded detectives and steamed away, leaving the invaders with no means of escape.

This battle lasted from four o'clock in the morning of July 6 until five o'clock that afternoon. Three Pinkertons and seven workers were killed, and many were wounded on both sides. Only after a dramatically moving speech by Hugh O'Donnell did the workers agree to accept a surrender of the Pinkertons, who were to be handed over to the sheriff on charges of murder. As the Pinkertons marched unarmed from the barges to the skating rink of the town, where they were to be kept, they were attacked and badly beaten, mostly by women. The crowd also seized the guns and provisions left behind and burned the barges.

Six days later, on July 12, eight thousand state militia men, mobilized by the governor of Pennsylvania upon Frick's appeal for aid, marched quietly to take control of Homestead and place it under martial law. With such protection the Carnegie Company began bringing in scabs and proceeded to file charges of rioting and murder against the strike leaders for the attack on the Pinkertons. The plant was reopened with militia protection, and nonunion men were given the Amalgamated members' jobs. When the strike was officially called off in November, two thousand strikebreakers had been brought in and only eight hundred of the original Homestead working force of nearly four thousand were reinstated.

This strike was surely one of the most violent in labor history. Each party to the dispute had taken the law into its own hands. In the end, however, the aggrieved remained aggrieved because government cherished law and order before justice.

Following the bloodshed at Homestead in 1892 a severe depression struck the nation in 1893. As the depression deepened, labor unrest grew more widespread, and a number of bitter strikes took place in various parts of the country. In the years following the railroad strikes of

1877 there arose many local conflicts between the railroad companies and their workers, but it was not until 1894 that a major conflict developed between these two parties, a conflict which turned into bitter violence before it was resolved.[22]

The setting for this struggle was the town of Pullman, some twelve miles south of Chicago. Established by the head of the company, it was described in its own brochures as a model. All the land and buildings in the town were the property of the Pullman Company. The plant—the factories, foundry, shops, steel mills—stood on two hundred acres. Another one hundred acres were covered with houses, apartments, and public structures such as a hotel, post office, bank, church, and an arcade of stores. Here the company regulated with paternal solicitude the lives of its employees and conducted its highly profitable business of manufacturing and repairing its cars, which were operated under contract on a hundred and twenty-five thousand miles of railroad, three-fourths of the total mileage of the country. Here the company was both employer and landlord for more than five thousand workers, who with their families and a few shopkeepers made up the population of twelve thousand. As their landlord the company collected rent, supplied water and gas, disposed of the sewage, accepted their savings in its bank, and rented books to them from its library. The workers, however, were dissatisfied with the setup: rents were high and so was the cost of services.

But in spite of their general discontent there was no organized resentment until the depression of 1893, when the company was briefly hard hit and laid off more than three thousand of its employees. It cut wages twenty-five percent, although the salaries of officers and managers remained the same and dividends were actually increased. To keep the plant operating, the company had taken contracts at a price less than the cost of labor and materials. After business began to improve, the company took back some two thousand of its employees, but no steps were taken to restore the wage cuts or reduce the rents.

After a long winter full of hardship, the resentment of the men came to a head, and in May, 1894, a committee of employees asked for some consideration of their grievances, particularly restoration of the wage scales to the level prior to the cuts of the preceding summer. Pullman flatly refused to consider either wage adjustments or rent reductions, and what is more, the company laid off three members of the grievance committee, in violation of its own promise. This triggered the men to act. That evening the men, most of whom were members of the American Railway Union, voted to strike. Six hundred of the nonunion workers were immediately laid off and the plant was closed.

In June delegates from around the nation gathered in Chicago for the convention of the American Railway Union. This union had been formed only the year before by Eugene V. Debs as an industrial union open to all white employees of the railroads. Its growth had been phenomenal: there were already a hundred and fifty thousand members. The Pullman employees had joined the union a little more than a month before the strike occurred.

They were considered eligible for membership on the grounds that the company had a fifty-mile railway at Pullman with its own engines, shops, and yard.

At the convention, committees were chosen to meet with the Pullman officials to persuade them to agree to arbitration. George M. Pullman himself met this overture with the uncompromising statement that "there is nothing to arbitrate." On June 21 the union adopted a resolution that if by June 26 the company remained unwilling to arbitrate the dispute, the members of the union would not handle Pullman cars. Such a strike by the Pullman employees would affect the entire railway system.

The challenge of the union was taken up by the General Managers' Association, a group of executives representing the twenty-four railways entering Chicago which together controlled some forty thousand miles of track. At a meeting with an officer of the Pullman Company on June 22, the Managers' Association resolved to "act unitedly" in resisting the boycott. Once the strike was effected, a strike headquarters was established and provision made for hiring men in place of those who were fired. The Managers' Association began to import strikebreakers from Canada, secretly instructing them to attach mail cars to Pullman cars so that when the strikers cut out the latter, they could be accused of interfering with the mails. Conjuring up a still nonexistent danger of violence, it induced Attorney General Olney to have thirty-four hundred men, who were actually hired and paid by the railroads, sworn in as special deputies to help keep the trains running. These tactics were successful. There were clashes between strikers and deputies; rioting broke out and railway property was destroyed. Promptly asserting that such violence had already become uncontrollable, the Managers' Association then appealed to President Cleveland to send federal troops to restore order, safeguard the mails, and protect interstate commerce.

Even though there had been no request from Governor Altgeld of Illinois or the legislature of the state, President Cleveland ordered out the federal troops, giving the reasons stated by the Managers' Association. "If it takes every dollar in the Treasury and every soldier in the United States to deliver a postal card in Chicago," he was reported as saying, "that postal card shall be delivered."

On July 4 four companies of the Fifteenth Infantry marched into Chicago and camped on the lakefront. By the following day there were nearly two thousand federal troops in Chicago under the command of General Miles, who established his headquarters in the Pullman building at Michigan Avenue and Adams Street.

The use of the federal troops stirred up violence that same day, on July 5. When the troops tried to help move the first train of Swift & Company meats from the Union stockyards, a crowd blocked the tracks and refused to leave until driven away by bayonet and cavalry charges. That night Mayor Hopkins issued a proclamation forbidding riotous assemblies, and Governor Altgeld, upon the mayor's application, ordered out the five regiments of militia stationed at Chicago. The city was now a military camp, with at least fourteen thousand men under arms. For the first time since the boycott was called, serious street fighting broke out. During the evening a colossal fire engulfed the buildings of the 1892 World's Columbian Exposition at Jackson Park. The overworked fire department was being summoned here and there where freight cars were blazing, and seven buildings were reduced to ashes before the fire was brought under control.

The peak of destruction was reached on Friday, July 6, when mobs destroyed railroad property worth more than one and a quarter million dollars at today's values. By this time hundreds of freight cars which had been stopped on various tracks were grouped together in the individual companies' yards, where they could more easily be guarded by the federal soldiers and the state militiamen. These yards were in the southern sections of the city, generally removed from any concentrations of buildings or houses. But the very extent of the long rows lining the tracks of the various sidings made car-to-car guarding impossible and led to a "carnival of incendiarism." The axle boxes of the freight cars were filled with greasy rags and waste; anyone could hide himself between or in the cars when a guard passed, then remove this waste, apply a match, and possess an ideal torch.

Because the day was breezy, it was not even necessary to set each car afire; the wind fanned the flames through the tightly packed cars. Since the fire hoses were seldom able to reach the line of flames, complete destruction was achieved with a minimum of activity.

The greatest destruction of freight cars in a single yard took place that night, when fires destroyed more than seven hundred cars in the Panhandle yards at Fiftieth Street in South Chicago. The yard was one of the largest—two miles long and a half-mile wide—and the tracks were packed solidly with freight cars. The mob there was said to have numbered six thousand. The Chicago *Inter-Ocean* reported the mob's work:

> From this moving mass of shouting rioters squads of a dozen or two departed, running towards the yards with fire brands in their hands. They looked in the gloaming like specters, their lighted torches bobbing about like will-o'-the-wisps. Soon from all parts of the yard flames shot up and billows of fire rolled over the cars, covering them with the red glow of destruction. The spectacle was a grand one . . . Before the cars were fired those filled with any cargoes were looted . . . The people were bold, shameless, and eager in their robbery . . . It was pandemonium let loose, the fire leaping along for miles and the men and women dancing with frenzy. It was a mad scene where riot became wanton and men and women became drunk on their excesses.[23]

Up to this time most of the casualties had been inflicted by the federal marshals and troops. However, since Governor Altgeld had called out the militia earlier in the day, the militiamen had been pouring into the city. They were now scattered throughout Chicago in small companies for the purpose of clearing the tracks, protecting railroad property, and restoring order.

This action precipitated the most violent encounter of the entire Chicago strike period. On the afternoon of July 7, while providing protection for a wrecking train on the Grand Trunk Line at Forty-ninth and Loomis streets, a company of the Illinois National Guard was attacked by an angry mob. A contemporary account described the scene:

Several thousand people had been following the train, and, as their number increased, many became bolder. Approaching Loomis Street, the train halted to raise a car which had been overturned. The crowd hooted and swore at the soldiers, throwing stones and bricks. A few shots were fired. After warning the crowd to disperse, the commander ordered his troops to load their rifles. For the moment this seemed to have a salutary effect, causing a few women and children to leave, but in reality generating an uglier spirit among the rioters. The hail of stones continued without interruption.

A bayonet charge was immediately ordered, during which some rioters were severely wounded. However, this cleared the railroad right of way. More determined than ever to resist the progress of the train, the mob returned, some of whom rushed forward and upset a flat car which had just been righted. More missiles were hurled and some shots fired by the rioters. Four soldiers had already been severely wounded and the lieutenant injured in the head by a stone. No reinforcements had appeared. The situation was perilous; there seemed to be no alternative left to the commanding officer except to order his men to fire at will and to make every shot count.[24]

The volleys resulted in the death of four rioters. About twenty more were wounded, including some women. Stunned, the crowd dispersed. The Loomis Street confrontation was the height of the Chicago violence. It was also the first time federal troops had fired on workers.

Under pressure of a Presidential proclamation and the presence of over fourteen thousand law-enforcement personnel—including city police, state militia, and federal troops—the strikers, their resistance weakened, returned to their jobs when the Pullman shops reopened on August 2. In all, the toll of this strike was twenty-five persons killed and sixty seriously injured. After the violence had died down, President Cleveland appointed a strike commission to study the Pullman Strike.[25] The commission made a number of recommendations, among them that compulsory arbitration be established and that labor organizations be recognized and dealt with by employers. These recommendations were never effected.

While only the Chicago phase of the nationwide strike has been described here, there was violence throughout most of the West and Southwest. The Northeast was not affected because Pullman did not hold contracts with those lines. After it was all over, however, labor had gained very little, and so there was no reason to hope that violence would diminish in the area of labor-management relations.

During the last decade of the nineteenth century large-scale violence continued to mark labor's struggle for recognition and for better wages and working conditions. A strike of metal miners in the Coeur d'Alene, Idaho, in 1892, resulted in the demolition of one of the mines and the deaths of several strikers and strikebreakers. Seven years later even more serious outbreaks of violence followed a strike call in the same region. Strikers seized a train, assaulted the workers, and dynamited a major mine, the Bunker Mill Mine. At the conclusion of this "successful" operation, the strikers were satisfied that the Bunker Mill operators would recognize their union after the mine was rebuilt and started operations and functioning again. They didn't. The violence gained nothing for the local of the Western Federation of Miners. All workers hired and rehired by the operators were screened and had to sign affidavits swearing that they had no affilia-

tion with the miners' union. A few years later Governor
Frank Steunenberg, who had broken the Coeur d'Alene
strike and had continued to crack down on miners' strikes
throughout his administration, was killed by a bomb
thrown by a professional assassin hired by the union.[26]

The early part of the twentieth century did not see any
end to violence in the labor movement. Conflict in the
Coeur d'Alene was dwarfed by events in Colorado, where
strikes in the metal-mining district in the 1880's and 1890's
had occasionally been accompanied by violence requiring
intervention of state troops and deputy sheriffs. These
strikes, however, could not compare with the one which
raged throughout the Cripple Creek area of Colorado
between 1903 and 1904. Dynamiting on two different
occasions resulted in the deaths of over twenty-six men
and the maiming of others. One incident was charged to
the union and the other to the operators. The governor
proclaimed Teller County, in which the Cripple Creek
area was located, to be in a state of insurrection; and the
writ of habeas corpus was suspended. Military rule was
lifted near the end of 1904, after many miners and their
sympathizers had been deported to Kansas and New
Mexico, or otherwise dispersed. The violent tactics used
by the strikers and the operators reflected the influence
of the frontier mentality which both sides shared.[27]

In the next year, 1905, the revolutionary-oriented Industrial Workers of the World was organized as a national
labor union. The I.W.W. was in effect the offspring of the
Western Federation of Miners. It was this militant miners'
union that contributed most of the financial and moral
support to set in motion the machinery of the larger union.

By no coincidence did the I.W.W. come into existence hard on the heels of the strike terrors of Cripple Creek.

From 1905 to 1920 the "Wobblies," as I.W.W. members were called, led some of the most violent strikes in American labor history.[28] Wherever one turned in this period, the Wobblies were leading in the battles of lumbermen, copper miners, agricultural workers, textile workers, even newsboys and Western Union messengers. But they were more often the victims of violence than its perpetrators.

The preamble of the I.W.W. began with the words, "The working class and the employing class have nothing in common" and this was an accurate summation of the ideology of the I.W.W., the most revolutionary union in American history. Many Americans believed it to be a criminal organization, its members freely practicing sabotage, destroying farm crops, and burning down buildings. The Wobblies were regarded as troublemakers and outlaws, the Ishmaelites of the industrial world, and they were treated or mistreated accordingly.

The widespread antagonism against the union was greatly increased when the United States entered World War I. The Wobblies opposed the war, contending that it held out nothing of value for labor, that it was a war of capitalists. To them there was only one legitimate war, the struggle to liberate the working class. Their organization was completely uninterested in national aims and purposes, and felt no loyalty to the government. Thus the hostility toward the organization was based on two distinct factors, the one economic and industrial, the other political. Attempts at suppression of the I.W.W. became violent, and the organization and its members were ostracized to such an extent that they had difficulty getting even legal redress of their grievances.

Probably the best-known strike led by the I.W.W. was the one at Lawrence, Massachusetts, where textile workers went on strike in 1912.[29] Twenty-three thousand workers were involved. The immediate cause of the strike was a cut in wages resulting from state legislation which reduced the hours of work for women and children under eighteen years of age from fifty-six to fifty-four hours per week.

During the period of the strike many acts of violence were committed by both the strikers and the deputies, police, and militiamen. One observer noted that at five o'clock in the morning on January 29, when it was still dark, a mob of strikers and their sympathizers attacked several streetcars, pulling the trolleys off the feed wire, smashing the windows with chunks of ice, driving off the motormen and conductors, and forbidding some passengers to leave the cars while throwing others into the streets. However, only a month later, on February 24, police attacked a group of women and children about to board a train for Philadelphia, clubbing them mercilessly. The brutal incident brought widespread support for the Lawrence strikers, and within a few weeks the American Woolen Company capitulated and granted all the workers' demands.

But the I.W.W. was much better at stirring things up than at organizing unions, and by the time the World War rolled around, the movement was on the downgrade. It played a fitting finale to its militancy when it opposed the participation of the

United States in the war and paid the price for it in jail sentences, terror, ostracism, and eventually destruction.[30]

A strike of coal miners in Colorado in 1913 became one of the major episodes of violence in this period. This strike was not so much a fight for higher wages or better working conditions as it was a revolt against political, economic, and social despotism.[31] The following contemporary analysis offers some graphic descriptions of the event as well as insights into its significance:

On the day of the capture of Vera Cruz, with a loss of four American lives, there came news of a battle in the State of Colorado which, as a Pittsburgh editor points out, "lasted longer and was more fiercely fought than most of the battles of the Mexican revolution." Correspondents of the great newspapers and press agencies had not been sent to Las Animas and Huerfano counties in throngs to report the details of the fighting, to check up the lists of casualties, and to account for the outbreak of hostilities. So we do not know whether the slaughter at Ludlow was "the blunder of a plain fool" or an incident in a "war of extermination," to cite two phrases used by Denver editors. We do know that last week's dispatches reported armed conflict between strikers and militiamen and guards, the burning of the Ludlow camp, where strikers lived with their families, attacks on mines and a twelve-mile-long line held for days by hundreds of miners against fewer but better-armed militiamen. This meant about two score dead, for the most part women and children, many of them burned and suffocated in the pits of refuge beneath their flame-swept tents; it meant as many others wounded or missing. The conservative New York *Evening Post,* shocked at such "savage play of brute passions," observes that "Victoriano Huerta might well prefer to sever relations with a Government under which it is possible for women and children to be mowed down by machine guns in a frenzy of civil war." The Mexican people, comments the Socialist New York *Call,* "would be foolish not to resist to their uttermost strength the friendly advances of a Government which prates of liberty and justice and then refuses to protect its own citizens from the murderous attacks of an organized band of Christian bandits." Other editors admit the seriousness of the Colorado situation, declare that civilized Government has broken down in that State, and call for Federal intervention.

It is as yet impossible to fix the responsibility for last week's outbreak. Conditions have for months been favorable for such an occurrence. . . . the chief bone of contention is the question of union recognition.

As for the fighting which began on the 20th, says the Denver *Mining and Financial Record,* it is important that the State of Colorado should "definitely discover whether this affair has been of an administrative nature, the work of a private corporation, or the blunder of a plain fool." According to Lieutenant Governor Fitzgerald "the trouble was started by the strikers killing a non-union man whose only offense was in walking to his work without their permission." Others assert that the militiamen shot a striker.

However the battle started, it soon spread over an area of about three square miles, according to the press dispatches, with about 200 militia opposed to an army of miners twice as large. At the Ludlow tent camp of the strikers, machine-guns were used by the militiamen. The camp took fire, perhaps from the shooting. "In the holes which had been dug for their protection against the rifles' fire, the women and children died like rats when the flame swept over them," says one account. After fourteen hours of fighting the camp was abandoned, and most of the women and children were taken to Trinidad.

Then came news of the constant growth of the strikers' army, their taking up positions on the hills surrounding the position taken by the militia, and of lives lost in attacks and sorties. Several mineshafts were attacked and burned. The exact loss of life is yet to be made known. Additional militiamen have been hurried from Denver, tho many refused to go, declaring that they would not fight women and children. The State Federation of Labor has called its members to arms in defense of the miners.

A vivid characterization of the Ludlow fight is given by the Denver *Express*, which has favored the mineworkers:

> Mothers and babies were crucified at Ludlow on the cross of human liberty. They tried to help their men folk rise in Rockefeller-ruled southern Colorado. Their crucification was effected by the operators' paid gunmen who have worn militia uniforms less than a week. The dead will go down in history as the hero victims of the burnt offering laid on the altar of Rockefeller's great god greed. With the operators enlisting gunfighters in Denver to-day, the end is not in sight.

Thus has been precipitated, says *The New York Times*, "a situation more grave than that which exists between this country and Mexico." As the New York *World* puts it, "The State of Colorado has gone out of business. Its paramount duty is to rehabilitate itself." Other Eastern papers declare it is time for the nation to act. The Federal Government, remarks the New York *Evening Mail*, will have to spare enough regular troops from Mexico "to restore peace and order in Colorado." . . .

In labor circles a large portion of the blame for what has happened in Colorado is laid to the door of John D. Rockefeller, Jr., and Mrs. Mary C. C. Bradford said at a Denver meeting:

> While Colorado is disgracing herself in the eyes of the world, the man who is responsible sits in his office in New York City. He is John D. Rockefeller, Jr. His statements before the Congress committee not only emboldened the weak and criminally disposed soldiers in the State, but they caused the miners to arm for war to the death because they realized what his remarks would bring forth.

It will be remembered that when Mr. Rockefeller was examined by Chairman Foster, of the House Committee on Mines and Mining, he admitted that the Rockefeller interests owned 40 per cent of the Colorado Fuel and Iron Company's stock. Several newspapers, omitting the intervening questions, quote as follows the most important part of Mr. Rockefeller's testimony:

> I have done what I regard as best in the interests of the employees and the large investment I represent. We have put the best obtainable men in charge, and are relying on their judgment. My conscience entirely acquits me. We would rather that the unfortunate conditions should continue, and that we should lose all the millions invested, than that American workmen should be deprived of their right, under the Constitution, to work for whom they please. That is the great principle at stake. It is a national issue.

When asked whether he could not go to Colorado and do something to end the killings, Mr. Rockefeller replied, according to the New York *Tribune:* "There is only one thing that could be done, and that is to unionize the mines, and we will not do that at any cost." "Mother" Jones has declared before the same commitee that "the strike will not end until the Rockefeller interests recognize the union."[32]

The definite refusal of the Rockefeller interests to grant the request of the President of the United States to arbitrate the sanguinary strike in Colorado brings up again sharply the right of labor and capital to carry on private wars, with sieges, battles, and loss of life. The battles were supposedly between the strikers and the State militia, the latter trying to preserve the peace, but the Colorado Springs *Gazette,* which is on the spot, throws a vivid light on the character of the State troops when it remarks that "we must purge our militia of gunfighters and murderers," and furthermore, "we must take our militia away forever from the clutches of big interests." . . .

The news accounts put the number of lives lost during the days of shooting and burning as high as 175 or as low as 72. This war, according to a Denver dispatch to the New York *Herald,* has cost the State of Colorado $750,000 in actual expenses and a business loss of more than $12,000,000. It has cost the United Mine Workers about $1,000,000, and the mine-owners $2,300,000 "in actual expense fighting the strikers," while their business loss is thought to amount to perhaps $10,000,000. At the coroner's inquest over the bodies of the twenty-five victims of the Ludlow battle, including fourteen children and two women, no evidence was brought out to show the immediate cause of the first shooting or the precise manner in which the tent colony was set on fire. . . . The Denver *Rocky Mountain News* prints half a dozen affidavits of men who saw the militia train their guns on the tents at Ludlow, and shoot at "anything they saw move, even a dog."[33]

Strikes for union recognition, almost always characterized by violence on both sides, continued year after year through the 1930's and the New Deal, by which time public legislation guaranteed labor's rights. In 1910 and 1911 violence occurred in Chicago, Cleveland, and New York during the clothing workers' strikes for recognition. It was the men's clothing strike in Chicago in 1910 which was the most violent. The strike began on September 12 as a protest against piece-work rate reductions. Spreading quickly, it engulfed the entire Chicago industry. Employers refused to meet with the strike committee, and only after 133 days was the newly organized union granted limited recognition. The industry had hired private detectives to escort strikebreakers, and they were involved in several shootings in which pickets were killed or wounded. During the strike seven were killed, unknown numbers seriously injured, and almost eight hundred and fifty arrests made.

After World War I a series of violent strikes took place in a number of industries. Expansion of union membership during the war had been reluctantly tolerated. Several million new recruits to the union movement were awaiting the end of the war to make further demands upon their employers. One of the most violent postwar encounters was in the steel industry, and again it was for union recognition. Led by the United States Steel Corporation, the industry refused to make any concessions on the issue of union recognition. A strike was called on September 22, 1919, and the overwhelming majority of production employees responded.

Clashes between the police and strikers were the rule. In Gary, Indiana, federal troops were requested after a clash between strikers and strikebreakers in the second week of the strike. The worst excesses were in Pennsylvania. Organizers were driven out of town during the organizing campaign and the strike. Meetings were suppressed, strikers were beaten, and strike activities impeded. Twenty people, eighteen of them strikers, perished in the strike, and many more suffered serious injuries.

The 1920's, otherwise known as the years of "normalcy," offered their share of bloody labor disputes. The coal miners' union never succeeded in drawing the major West Virginia fields into the central competitive field. Operating from a more favorable competitive position as a result of their ability to keep the union off their territory, major producers in West Virginia were determined to prevent unionization of their properties.

In May, 1920, trouble started between some of the newly organized Union miners and company guards in Mingo and McDowell counties. In one of the towns, while Baldwin-Felts agents were evicting a union miner, an argument developed between the guards and the miners, the sheriff, and the mayor during which ten died from gunshot wounds. In another battle between guards and strikers in Mingo County, on August 21, 1920, six were reported killed. The governor requested federal troops, and their presence brought an end to the rioting. A large number of deputy sheriffs were appointed, which made it possible to withdraw the troops, but their departure brought a renewal of violence. In December, 1920, the prosecuting attorney of Mingo County attributed sixteen killings directly to the strike at the Mingo County mines.

A Senate committee found that both sides were guilty of acts of violence, and that those committed by the United Mine Workers' Union were "absolutely indefensible. Men have been killed, property destroyed, telephone wires cut, trains commandeered and misused, a march of some thousands of men organized and policies carried out which bordered close on insurrection."

The Coal Commission somewhat irrelevantly noted that almost all of the nonunion counties "were almost exclusively peopled by mountaineers—native whites of ancient American ancestry. Their annals are crimson with feuds and the gun was the 'supreme court' . . ." Much of the violence had nothing to do with the national or racial characteristics of the people, yet they provided both sides with excellent grounds for initiating arguments.

Two years later another section of the country—the state of Illinois—was the scene of one of the bloodiest episodes on record in American labor history. The Southern Illinois Coal Company, located in the Town of Herrin, had negotiated unsuccessfully with the local union prior to the general strike of April, 1922, and its employees joined the walkout. After two weeks the company, with the permission of the union, began stripping the surface. Later the company broke relations with the union and began mining coal. Those brought in to do the mining were members of an independent union which John L. Lewis described as an "outlaw organization," meaning a dual, unaffiliated union. When the local miners attempted to confer with their replacements, they were greeted with gunfire, and two of the unionists were killed. The killings were the work of guards brought in by William J. Lester, who controlled the company, to protect the mining operations. Lester had been warned of the danger of his strategy by the sheriff of Williamson County, in which Herrin was located, but he had disregarded the advice. A stockade was put up to protect the mines, and later in June a contingent of armed miners stormed the stockade after spraying it with rifle fire. The men behind the wall surrendered, and they were beaten and shot. Eighteen guards and strikebreakers, including Lester, died in that assault, making it a total of twenty-one who were killed in this attempt to break the union.[34]

After 1923 the number of strikes dropped sharply, but sporadic violence occurred during several labor disputes. At the end of the decade of the twenties there was a series of textile strikes which resulted in deaths of seven persons amid clashes between pickets and strikers, and strikers and police.

For the past four and a half years the United States has been in the throes of a major labor upheaval, which can fairly be described as one of the greatest mass movements in our history.

There has been labor unrest ever since there was a factory system, but the movement here can properly be traced back to 1866–87, a period of open warfare characterized for the first time by a series of important strikes on the issue of the right to organize and bargain collectively through nationwide unions. The claim to that right, now widely conceded in Britain and the European democracies but still resisted in the United States, is the keystone of the American labor movement—is indeed what dignifies it as a movement rather than an intermittent and aimless war.[35]

Again a nationwide economic depression, this time the most devastating in American history, gave rise to an explosive social climate in America. During the four-year period of the Great Depression, May, 1933, to July, 1937, there were some ten thousand strikes drawing out over five million workers.

This was aside from all the thousands of quickies, sitdowns, and other protests that tied up industry during that period— a "strike" as defined by the Department of Labor and used in this article, being an affair involving at least six workers for at least one day.[36]

The national cotton-textile strike was probably the most violent labor dispute of the early thirties, a period marked by violent clashes throughout the nation. Textile workers averaged eleven dollars a week. In June, 1934, the cotton-textile code authority established by the New Deal reduced production by twenty-five percent. This meant a sharp cut in wages. Picket lines of members new to organized labor tightened around hundreds of the industry's mills, and they stopped production so effectively that textile trade papers reported that the employers felt they had been outgeneraled by an "audacious and intelligent minority." In the South, during the first week of the strike, fifty "flying squadrons" of pickets (flying squadrons were groups of strikers in automobiles who descended on towns suddenly and unexpectedly), with from two hundred to six hundred and fifty men in each column of cars, were operating along a one-hundred-and-ten-mile front from Gastonia to Grenville in the Carolinas. At Trion, Georgia, a deputy sheriff, a picket, and a strike sympathizer were killed and fifteen strikers were wounded in a pitched battle. At Grenville another strike sympathizer was killed, and during the strike's course there were clashes between pickets, deputies, nonstrikers, and guardsmen as far apart as Woonsocket, Rhode Island; Lancaster, Pennsylvania; and Augusta, Georgia, where three more strikers were shot, one fatally. At the gate of the Chiquola Manufacturing Company's plant at Honea Path, South Carolina, a group of armed men opposing the strike opened fire on the picket line as they charged it, killing six pickets and wounding fifteen. More than ten thousand national guardsmen were arrayed against the strikers in eight states, and a concentration camp for pickets had been set up in Georgia.[37] The strike ended on September 22 when the union leaders asked President Roosevelt to end the walkout, which had developed into a battle far greater than the union could handle. Union members were not rehired, and membership by August, 1935, was 79,200, a drop of more than 220,000 from its high point in the summer of 1934.

The Little Steel Strike in 1937 was another of the major

incidents of violence during this period of the Depression and the early days of the New Deal.

> Read the report of the La Follette Committee on what it calls the Memorial Day incident and you will find a story as savage as any in the dark annals of American labor struggles. . . .
>
> You will read also of the marchers approaching the line of 264 police, of a discussion about picketing suddenly interrupted by a stick thrown by the inevitable unknown, a tear-gas bomb tossed at the moment the cameraman was changing his lenses, and, after a graphic report of the subsequent gunfire, the brutal treatment of the injured, and the sixty-seven arrests, the grim conclusion that "the consequences of the Memorial Day encounter were clearly avoidable by the police."[38]

Farmers as well as factory workers resorted to violence in their desperation during this era of economic depression. Income for the farmers skidded to new lows by falling nearly seventy-five percent. Farmers found it impossible to meet their mortgage obligations, and most of them confronted the dreaded foreclosure proceedings. Like the farmers in western Massachusetts and western Pennsylvania during the early days of the republic, farmers from Bucks County, Pennsylvania, to Antelope County, Nebraska, banded together to stop banks and insurance companies from dispossessing them of their land. When sheriffs attempted to carry out foreclosures, mobs of farmers, brandishing pitchforks and dangling hangman's nooses, forced the sheriffs to retreat. Marches on the courthouses coupled with threats of personal violence against the judges themselves were common. In the dairy states farmers engaged in violent activities to prevent milk from getting to market in a vain effort to force up prices.[39]

The president of the Farmers' Union of Wisconsin told a Senate committee:

> They are just ready to do anything to get even with the situation. I almost hate to express it, but I honestly believe that if some of them could buy airplanes they would come down here to Washington to blow you fellows up. . . .[40]

For the first time Lloyd's of London sold large sums of "riot and civil commotion insurance" to Americans. All over the country during the first years of the crash, bread lines lengthened in the cities, and the mood of the country grew ugly. In July, 1931, unemployed men stormed food shops in various parts of the nation; hunger marchers paraded in almost every major city.

The violence and the threat of violence during this period in America's history forced the "haves" in American society to recognize the fact that they could ignore the plight of the masses of native Americans only at their own peril. These episodes of rebellion sensitized the government and the establishment community to the need for social and economic reconstruction. They listened to the voices of discontent and accommodated themselves to the desperation acted out by the people. The result of this accommodation was the New Deal, which probably prevented the disintegration of American society at that point.

Norman Thomas, always an advocate of nonviolence in the pursuit of social change, had conceded that violence

. . . may be terribly costly, but it has gotten results. In moderate doses . . . it has been publicity for the underdog. It also serves as warning that he may have power. Slaves content to be slaves, workers content to starve quietly, never get deliverance from heaven or from sheer human kindness. And the natural vehicle of their protest, especially given our Western traditions (quite unlike the Indian tradition to which Gandhi has appealed), is some degree of violence. No honest and intelligent person can say that in our imperfect democracy we have a polite and easy substitute for violence in the right to organize unions and to vote. The most we can say is that there is a power in them not adequately asserted by the workers of America. Ballots are better than bullets and an organized strike than a riot. The history of such considerable labor violence as was used by the Molly Maguires, the Pittsburgh and Baltimore rioters of the seventies, and the dynamiters in Los Angeles, is a history of a great setback for labor. It was not altogether useful publicity for the underdog! Yet he lacks imagination who does not see why the harassed worker or striker, seeing his job taken and his struggle defeated by a scab under police protection, finding himself evicted, perhaps at night, from his home, takes to himself a stone, a club, or a gun rather than a ballot. No exploited class can afford to let the masters think it will not use violence unless it can discover a more effective instrument of struggle than violence. . . . For workers merely to renounce violence with no substitute in sight would be to play into the hands of the oppressor.[41]

The implications of Thomas' message for the discontented segments of American society today clearly suggests the challenge which confronts the power structure.

NOTES

1. For the most detailed and documented study of this incredible year of violence, see Robert V. Bruce, *1877: Year of Violence* (Indianapolis, 1959).
2. See O. V. Wells, "The Depression of 1873–79," *Agricultural History*, Vol. XI (1937).
3. This account is drawn from Herbert G. Gutman, "The Tompkins Square Riot in New York City," *Labor History*, Vol. II (Winter, 1955), pp. 44–70.
4. Quoted in *ibid.*, p. 51.
5. *Ibid.*, p. 63.
6. *Ibid.*, p. 66.
7. A quaintly biased "history" of the Maguires appears in James D. McCabe (pseudonym, Edward W. Martin) *The History of the Great Riots* (Philadelphia, 1877).
8. See *The New York Times*, December 7, 1947.
9. Quoted in McCabe, *op. cit.*, p. 24.
10. See Bennett M. Rich, *The Presidents and Civil Disorders* (Washington, D.C., 1941).
11. Baltimore *Evening Bulletin*, July 7, 1877.
12. McCabe, *op. cit.*, p. 63.
13. Quoted in *ibid.*, p. 79.
14. See Bruce, *op. cit.*, p. 141.
15. See *Report of the Committee Appointed to Investigate the*

Railroad Riots in July, 1877 (Harrisburg, Pennsylvania, 1878).

16. McCabe, *op. cit.*, pp. 91–92.

17. *Ibid.*, p. 102.

18. See Philip S. Foner, *History of the Labor Movement in the United States* (New York, 1947), pp. 468–469.

19. See Bruce, *op. cit.*, Chapter 10.

20. See Samuel Yellen, *American Labor Struggles* (New York, 1936), Chapter 2.

21. See Louis Adamic, *Dynamite: The Story of Class Violence in America* (New York, 1931), pp. 101–107; Foster R. Dulles, *Labor in America*, 2d rev. ed. (New York, 1960), pp. 166–171; Philip Taft, *Organized Labor in American History* (New York, 1964), pp. 136–145; Leon Wolff, *Lockout* (New York, 1965); and Samuel Yellen, *op. cit.*, pp. 72–100.

22. See Adamic, *op. cit.*, pp. 115–123; Dulles, *op. cit.*, 171–180; Almont Lindsey, *The Pullman Strike: The Story of a Unique Experiment and of a Great Labor Upheaval* (Chicago, 1942); Bennett, *op. cit.*, pp. 87–101; Taft, *op. cit.*, pp. 146–158; Colston E. Warne, *The Pullman Boycott of 1894* (New York, 1955); and Yellen, *op. cit.*, pp. 101–135.

23. Chicago *Inter Ocean*, July 7, 1894.

24. *Ibid.*, July 8, 1894.

25. See U.S. Senate, "Report on the Chicago Strike of June–July, 1894, by U.S. Strike Commission," 53d Cong, 3d sess., Ex. Doc. No. 7 (Washington, D.C., 1895).

26. See Adamic, *op. cit.*, pp. 124–127; George F. French, "Coeur d'Alene Riots, 1892," *Overland Monthly*, Vol. XXVI (1895), pp. 32–49; Leon Whipple, *The Story of Civil Liberty in the United States* (New York, 1939), pp. 238–241; and S. S. Boynton, "Miners' Vengeance," *Overland Monthly*, Vol. XXII (1893), pp. 303–307.

27. See U.S. Senate, "Report on the Labor Disturbances in the State of Colorado from 1880–1904," 58th Cong., 3d sess., Doc. No. 122 (Washington, D.C., 1905).

28. See Paul F. Brissenden, *The I.W.W.: A Study of American Syndicalism* (New York, 1919).

29. See Adamic, *op. cit.*, pp. 165–167; U.S. Senate, "Report on Strike of Textile Workers in Lawrence, Mass., in 1912,"

62d Cong., 2d sess., Doc. No. 870 (Washington, D.C., 1912); and U.S. House Report, "The Strike at Lawrence, Mass.," 62d Cong., 2d sess., Doc. No. 671 (Washington, D.C., 1912). See also L. F. Deland, "The Lawrence Strike: A Study," *The Atlantic Monthly*, Vol. CIX (1912), pp. 694–705.

30. Foner, *op. cit.*, p. 39.
31. See Yellen, *op. cit.*, Chapter 7.
32. *Literary Digest*, May 2, 1914, pp. 1033–1034.
33. *Ibid.*, May 9, 1914, pp. 1099–1100.
34. See Paul M. Angle, *Bloody Williamson* (New York, 1952).
35. "Industrial Warfare," *Fortune*, Vol. XVI (November, 1937), p. 109.
36. *Ibid.*, p. 105.
37. See Edward Levinson, *Labor on the March* (New York, 1938).
38. *Fortune, op. cit.*, p. 111.
39. See William E. Leuchtenburg, *The Perils of Prosperity: 1914–1932* (Chicago, 1958), pp. 261–262.
40. Quoted in *ibid.*, p. 262.
41. Norman Thomas, *As I See It* (New York, 1932), pp. 55–57.

BIBLIOGRAPHY

General

ADAM, JAMES T., "Our Lawless Heritage," *The Atlantic Monthly*, Vol. CXLV (1928), pp. 732–740.

BAKAL, CARL, *The Right to Bear Arms* (New York, 1966).

BELOFF, MAX, *Public Order and Popular Disturbances, 1660–1714* (London, 1938).

BERKOWITZ, LEONARD, *Aggression: A Social Psychological Analysis* (New York, 1962).

BETTLEHEIM, BRUNO, "Individual and Mass Behavior in Extreme Situations," *Journal of Abnormal and Social Psychology*, Vol. XXXVIII (1943), pp. 417–421.

BOSKIN, JOSEPH, "A History of Urban Conflicts in the 20th Century," in Audrey Rawitscher, compiler, *Riots in the City: An Addendum to the McCone Commission Report* (Los Angeles, 1967), pp. 1–24.

BRINTON, CRANE, *Anatomy of Revolution* (New York, 1952).

BUSS, ARNOLD H., *The Psychology of Aggression* (New York, 1961).

CADOUX, C. J., "Ethics of Coercion," *Contemporary Review*, Vol. XCLV (1934), pp. 688–697.

CALHOUN, J. B., "Population Density and Social Pathology," in L. J. Duhl, ed., *The Urban Condition* (New York, 1963).

CARSTAIRS, GEORGE M., "Overcrowding and Human Aggression," *Violence in America: Historical and Comparative Perspectives,* National Commission on the Causes and Prevention of Violence (Washington, D.C., 1969), Vol. II, Chapter 21.

CONNERY, ROBERT H., ed., *Urban Riots: Violence and Social Change,* Proceedings of the Academy of Political Science, Vol. XXIX (1968).

COSER, LEWIS A., *The Functions of Social Conflict* (New York, 1956).

DAVIES, JAMES C., *When Men Revolt—And Why* (New York, 1969).

DEGLER, CARL, "Our Taste for Violence," *The Nation,* Vol. CLXI (1960), p. 94.

DOLLARD, JOHN, *Frustration and Aggression* (New Haven, 1939).

FANON, FRANZ, *The Wretched of the Earth* (New York, 1963).

FELLMAN, G. A., and ZIMBURG, N. E., "Violence and Biological Need and Social Control," *Social Forces,* Vol. XLV (1967), pp. 533–541.

FREUD, SIGMUND, *Civilization and Its Discontents,* James Strachey, ed. (New York, 1962).

GEIS, GEORGE, "Violence in American Society," *Current History,* Vol. LII (1967), pp. 354 ff.

GORER, GEOFFRY, "Man Has No 'Killer' Instinct," *The New York Times Sunday Magazine* (November 17, 1966).

GURR, TED R., "Urban Disorder: Perspectives from the Comparative Study of Civil Strife," in Louis H. Masott and Don R. Bowen, eds., *Riots and Rebellion: Civil Violence in the Urban Community* (Beverley Hills, California, 1968).

———— "Psychological Factors in Civil Violence," *World Politics,* Vol. XX (1968), pp. 245–278.

———— *Why Men Rebel* (Princeton, New Jersey, 1969).

HEADLEY, JOEL T., *The Great Riots of New York, 1712 to 1873* (New York, 1873).

HOLBROOK, STEWART H., "Our Tradition of Violence," *American Mercury,* Vol. XLVIII (1944), pp. 338–344.

IANNI, F. A. J., "Teaching Violence as a Means Toward Social Justice," *Catholic World,* Vol. CCVI (1968), pp. 160–164.

KRUTCH, JOHN W., "What Does Violence Say About Man?" *Saturday Review,* Vol. XLVII (1965), pp. 18–19.

LEVY, SHELDON G., "The Psychology of the Politically Violent," *Pacific Sociology Association* (Seattle, Washington, 1969).

LORENZ, KONRAD, *On Aggression* (New York, 1966).

LYNN, KENNETH, "Violence in American Literature and Folklore," *Violence in America: Historical and Comparative Perspectives,* National Commission on the Causes and Prevention of Violence (Washington, D.C., 1969), Vol. I, Chapter 6.

MASSOT, LOUIS H., ed., "Urban Violence and Disorder," *American Behavioral Science*, Vol. XI (1968), pp. 1–55.

MENNINGER, KARL, *Man Against Himself* (New York, 1938).

MILLER, WILLIAM R., *Nonviolence: A Christian Interpretation* (New York, 1964).

MONTAGUE, ASHLEY, ed., *Man and Aggression* (New York, 1968).

NIEBURG, H. L., "Threat of Violence and Social Change," *American Political Science Review*, Vol. LXVI (1962), pp. 865–873.

ORTEGA Y GASSETT, JOSE, *Revolt of the Masses* (New York, 1932).

PETEGORSKY, DAVID W., "Violence and Social Change," *Antioch Review*, Vol. I (1941), pp. 243–248.

RIFKIN, A. H., "Violence in Human Behavior," *Science*, Vol. CXL (1963), pp. 904–906.

RUDE, GEORGE F., *The Crowd in History: A Study of Popular Disturbances in France and England, 1730–1848* (New York, 1964).

SCHLESINGER, ARTHUR M., JR., *Violence: America in the Sixties* (New York, 1968).

SOREL, GEORGES, *Reflections on Violence* (New York, 1950).

TEGGART, F. J., "War and Civilization in the Future: Modern Thought Is Dominated by Theories of Violence," *American Journal of Sociology*, Vol. XLVI (1941), pp. 582–590.

"Violence," *Esquire*, Vol. LXVIII (July, 1967), pp. 39 ff.

"Violence," *20th Century*, Vol. CLXXIII (1964–1965), pp. 6–130.

"Violence in America," *Time*, Vol. XC (July 28, 1967), pp. 18–19.

"Violence in the Nation: Treatment, Particularly in the United States," *Psychological Review*, Vol. LI (1944), pp. 147–161.

"Violence Symposium," *The Nation*, Vol. CCV (1967), pp. 101–107.

WADE, RICHARD, "Violence in the Cities: An Historical View," *Urban Violence* (Chicago, 1969), pp. 7–26.

Wolfgang, Marvin E., ed., "Patterns of Violence: Symposium," *Annals of the American Academy of Political and Social Sciences*, Vol. CCCLXIV (1966).

Yates, Aubrey, J., *Frustration and Conflict* (New York, 1962).

Violence on the Indian Frontier

Beeson, John, *A Plea for the Indians* (New York, 1858).

Dunn, John P., *Massacres of the Mountains* (London, 1856).

Franklin, Benjamin, *Works of Benjamin Franklin*, John Bigelow, ed., Vol. IV, Federal Edition (New York, 1904).

Leach, Douglas E., *Flintlock and Tomahawk: New England in King Philip's War* (New York, 1966).

Macleod, William C., *The American Indian Frontier* (New York, 1928).

U.S. Senate, Reports of Committee, 39th Cong., 2d sess., Ser. 1279, Doc. No. 156 (Sand Creek Massacre, 1872).

Racial Violence

Aptheker, Herbert, *American Negro Slave Revolts* (New York, 1943).

Baker, Ray S., *Following the Color Line* (New York, 1908).

Beatly, George W., *The Background and Causes of the 1943 Detroit Race Riot* (Princeton, New Jersey, 1954).

Booth, Mary L., *History of the City of New York* (New York, 1880).

Brearley, H. C., "Pattern of Violence," in W. T. Couch, ed., *Culture in the South* (Chapel Hill, 1935).

Brown, Earl, "The Truth About the Detroit Race Riot," *Harper's Magazine*, Vol. CLXXXVII (1943), pp. 488–498.

Caldwell, Erskine, "The Deep South's Other Venerable Tradition," *The New York Times Sunday Magazine* (July 11, 1965).

Caplan, Nathan S., "A Study of Ghetto Rioters," *Scientific American*, Vol. CCXIX (1968), pp. 15–21.

Cohen, Nathan E., "The Los Angeles Riot Study," in Shalom Edleman, ed., *Violence in the Streets* (Chicago, 1968).

Comer, James P., "The Dynamics of Black and White Violence,"

Violence in America: Historical and Comparative Perspectives,
A Report Submitted to the National Commission on the Causes
and Prevention of Violence (New York, 1969), Chapter 11.

CROUTHAMEL, JAMES L., "Springfield Race Riot of 1908," *Journal
of Negro History,* Vol. XLV (1960), pp. 164–173.

CRUSE, HAROLD, *The Crisis of the Negro Intellectual* (New York,
1967).

CUTLER, JAMES E., *Lynch-Law: An Investigation into the History
of Lynching in the United States* (New York, 1905).

DOLLARD, JOHN, *Caste and Class in a Southern Town* (Garden
City, New York, 1949).

FRANKLIN, JOHN HOPE, *The Militant South* (Cambridge, Massachusetts, 1956).

——— *From Slavery to Freedom* (New York, 1967).

GRIMSHAW, ALLEN D., "A Study in Social Violence: Urban Race
Riots in the United States," unpublished Ph.D. dissertation
(University of Pennsylvania, 1959).

——— "Factors Contributing to Color Violence in the United
States and Great Britain," *Race* (May, 1962), pp. 18 ff.

——— "Actions of Police and Military in American Race Riots,"
Phylon (Winter, 1963), pp. 288 ff.

HAYDEN, TOM, *Rebellion in Newark: Official Violence and Ghetto
Response* (New York, 1967).

MCCAGUE, JAMES, *The Second Rebellion: The Study of the New
York City Draft Riots of 1863* (New York, 1968).

MECKLIN, JOHN M., *The Ku Klux Klan: A Study of the American
Mind* (New York, 1963).

MEIR, AUGUST, AND RUDWICK, ELLIOTT M., "Black Violence in the
20th Century: A Study in Rhetoric and Retaliation," *Violence
in America: Historical and Comparative Perspectives,* A Report
Submitted to the National Commission on the Causes and
Prevention of Violence (New York, 1969), Chapter 9.

MYERS, GUSTAVUS, *History of Bigotry in the United States* (New
York, 1960).

ORLANSKY, HAROLD, *The Harlem Riot: A Study in Mass Frustration* (New York, 1943).

PORTERFIELD, AUSTIN, "Indices of Suicide and Homicide by State
and Cities: Some Southern and Non-Southern Contrasts with
Implications for Research," *American Sociological Review,*
Vol. XIV (1949), pp. 481–490.

RAMAGE, BURR J., "Homicide in the Southern States," *Sewanee Review*, Vol. IV (1895–1896), pp. 221–230.

REDFIELD, H. V., *Homicide: North and South* (Philadelphia, 1880).

Report of the National Advisory Commission on Civil Disorders (New York, 1968).

RISTER, C. C., "Mob Violence in the Old South," *Mississippi Valley Historical Review*, Vol. XXIX (1942), pp. 351–370.

RUDWICK, ELLIOTT M., *Race Riot at East St. Louis: July 2, 1917* (Carbondale, Illinois, 1964).

SCHULER, EDGAR A., "The Houston Race Riot, 1917," *Journal of Negro History*, Vol. XXIX (1944), pp. 300–338.

SHOGAN, ROBERT, and CRAIG, TOM, *The Detroit Race Riot: A Study in Violence* (Philadelphia and New York, 1964).

SILVER, ALLEN, "Official Interpretations of Racial Riots," in Robert H. Conway, ed., *Urban Riots: Violence and Social Change*, Proceedings of the Academy of Political Science, Vol. XXIX (1968), pp. 146–158.

The Negro in Chicago: A Study of Race Relations and a Race Riot, Chicago Commission on Race Relations (Chicago, 1922).

"The Waco Horror," supplement to *The Crisis* (July, 1916).

WANDERER, JULES J., "1967 Riots: A Test of the Congruity of Events," *Social Problems*, Vol. XV (1968), pp. 193–198.

WILLIAMS, F., *Negroes With Guns* (New York, 1962).

WILLIAMS, ROBERT M., "Social Change and Social Conflict: Racial Relations in the United States, 1944–1964," *Social Inquiry* (April, 1965), pp. 8–25.

The Abolitionist Crusade

AMES, ELLIS, "Garrison Mob," *Proceedings of the Massachusetts Historical Society*, Vol. XVIII (1881), pp. 341 ff.

BEECHER, LYMAN, *Narrative of Riots at Alton: In Connection with the Death of Rev. Elijah P. Lovejoy* (Alton, 1838). Paperback edition published by E. P. Dutton (New York, 1965).

CHAPMAN, JOHN JAY, *William Lloyd Garrison* (Boston, 1921).

CURRY, RICHARD, ed., *Abolitionists: Reformers or Fanatics?* (New York, 1965).

DEMOS, J., "Antislavery Movement and Problems of Violent Means," *New England Quarterly*, Vol. XXXVII (1964), pp. 501–526.

DILLON, MERTON L., *Elijah P. Lovejoy, Abolitionist Editor* (Urbana, Illinois, 1961).

DUBERMAN, MARTIN B., ed., *The Antislavery Vanguard: New Essays on the Abolitionists* (Princeton, New Jersey, 1965).

EATON, CLEMENT, "Mob Violence in the Old South," *Mississippi Valley Historical Review*, Vol. XXIX (1943), pp. 351–370.

FILLER, LOUIS, *The Crusade Against Slavery* (New York, 1960).

GILL, JOHN, *Tide Without Turning: Elijah P. Lovejoy and Freedom of the Press* (Boston, 1958).

LADER, LAWRENCE, *The Bold Brahmins, New England's War Against Slavery* (New York, 1961).

RUCHAMES, LOUIS, ed., *The Abolitionists: A Collection of Their Writings* (New York, 1963).

WEISBERGER, BERNARD A., ed., *Abolitionism: Disrupter of the Democratic System or Agent of Progress?* (Chicago, 1963).

Political Authority and Resistance

BAILYN, BERNARD, ed., *Pamphlets of the American Revolution, 1750–1776*, Vol. I (Cambridge, Massachusetts, 1965).

BALDWIN, LELAND D., *Whiskey Rebels: The Story of a Frontier Uprising* (Pittsburgh, 1939).

BRIDENBAUGH, CARL, *Cities in the Wilderness* (New York, 1955).
——— *Cities in Revolt* (New York, 1955).

BROOKS, ROBIN, "Domestic Violence and America's Wars: An Historical Interpretation," *Violence in America: Historical and Comparative Perspectives*, A Report Submitted to the National Commission on the Causes and Prevention of Violence (New York, 1969), Chapter 15.

BROWN, RICHARD M., *The South Carolina Regulators* (Cambridge, Massachusetts, 1963).

CALVERT, PETER A. R., "Revolution: The Politics of Violence," *Political Studies*, Vol. XVL (1967), p. 1–9.

DAVIES, JAMES C., "The Circumstances and Causes of Revolution," *Journal of Conflict Resolution*, Vol. XI (1967), pp. 247–257.

FEIERABEND, IVO K. and ROSALIND L., and NESVOLD, BETTY A., "Social Change and Political Violence: Cross-National Patterns," *Violence in America: Historical and Comparative Perspectives*, A Report Submitted to the National Commission on the Causes and Prevention of Violence (New York, 1969), Chapter 18.

———— and NESVOLD, BETTY A., "Political Violence and Social Discontent," in David C. Schwartz, ed., *Revolution Studies* (in press).

HANSEN, MILLARD, "The Significance of Shays' Rebellion," *South Atlantic Quarterly*, Vol. VI (1933), pp. 99–130.

HOOKER, RICHARD J., ed., *The Carolina Backcountry on the Eve of the Revolution* (Chapel Hill, 1953).

JAMES, ALFRED P., "A Political Interpretation of the Whiskey Rebellion," *Western Pennsylvania History Magazine*, Vol. XXXIII (1950), pp. 90–101.

LABAREE, BENJAMIN W., *The Boston Tea Party* (New York, 1964).

LAQUER, WALTER, "Revolution," *International Encyclopedia of the Social Sciences*, Vol. XIII (New York, 1968).

LEMISCH, JESSE, "Jack Tar in the Streets: Merchant Seamen in Revolutionary America," *William and Mary Quarterly*, Vol. XXV (1968), pp. 371–407.

LEWIS, ANTHONY, *Portrait of a Decade* (New York, 1964).

LONGLEY, R. S., "Mob Activities in Revolutionary Massachusetts," *New England Quarterly*, Vol. VI (1933), p. 99–130.

MARK, IRVING, *Agrarian Conflicts in Colonial New York, 1711–1775* (New York, 1940).

MILLER, JOHN C., *Origins of the American Revolution* (Stanford, California, 1966).

MOODY, ROBERT E., "Samuel Ely: Forerunner of Shays," *New England Quarterly*, Vol. V (1932), pp. 105–134.

MORGAN, EDMUND S., ed., *Prologue to Revolution* (Chapel Hill, 1959).

———— and MORGAN, HELEN M., *The Stamp Act Crisis: Prologue to Revolution*, rev. ed. (New York, 1963).

PETERSON, H. C., and FITE, GILBERT C., *Opponents of War, 1917–1918* (Madison, Wisconsin, 1957).

RICH, BENNETT M., *The Presidents and Civil Disorder* (Washington, D.C., 1941).

RUDOLPH, LLOYD I., "The Eighteenth Century Mob in America

and Europe," *American Quarterly*, Vol. XI (1959), pp. 447–469.

SCHLESINGER, ARTHUR M., "Political Mobs and the American Revolution, 1765–1776," *American Philosophical Proceedings*, Vol. XCIX (1955), pp. 244–251.

SMITH, JONATHAN, "The Depression of 1785 and Daniel Shays' Rebellion," *American Antiquarian Society Proceedings*, Vol. XV (1902), pp. 200–232.

STARKEY, MARION L., *A Little Rebellion* (New York, 1955).

WADA, GEORGE, and DAVIES, JAMES C., "Riot and Rioters," *Western Political Quarterly*, Vol. X (1957), pp. 864–874.

WOOD, F. J., "Paper Money and Shays' Rebellion," *Stone & Webster Journal*, Vol. XXVI (1920).

WOOD, GORDON S., "A Note on Mobs in the American Revolution," *William and Mary Quarterly*, Vol. XXIII (1966), pp. 634–642.

The Anti-Catholic Tradition

"Anti-Catholic Movement in the United States," *Catholic World*, Vol. X (1875), pp. 810–813

BEALS, CARLETON, *Brass-Knuckle Crusade* (New York, 1960).

BILLINGTON, RAY S. *The Protestant Crusade* (Gloucester, Massachusetts, 1963).

McMASTER, JOHN B., *With the Fathers* (New York, 1896).

MYERS, GUSTAVUS, *History of Bigotry in the United States* (New York, 1943).

SCHMECKEBIER, LAURENCE F., *History of the Know-Nothing Party in Maryland*, Johns Hopkins University Studies in History and Political Science, Vol. XVII (Baltimore, 1899).

SHEA, JOHN D., *History of the Catholic Church in the United States*, Vol. IV (New York, 1886–1898).

SWEET, WILLIAM W., *Religion in Colonial America* (New York, 1942). "The Anti-Catholic Riots of 1844 in Philadelphia," *American Catholic Historical Researches*, Vol. XII (1896), pp. 50–64. *The Charlestown Convent: Its Destruction by a Mob on the Night of August 11, 1834; with a History of the Excitement before the Burning, and the Strange and Exaggerated Reports Relating Thereto, the Feeling of Regret and*

Indignation Afterwards; the Proceedings of Meetings, and Expressions of the Contemporary Press (Boston, 1870).

Mormons and the Nation

BROOKS, JUANITA, *The Mountain Meadows Massacre* (Norman, Oklahoma, 1962).

CREER, LELAND, *Utah and the Nation* (New York, 1929).

ELY, RICHARD T., "Economic Aspects of Mormonism," *Harper's Magazine*, Vol. CVI (1903), pp. 667–678.

FIFE, AUSTIN E., "A Ballad of the Mountain Meadows Massacre," *Western Folklore*, Vol. XII (October, 1953), pp. 229–241.

The Anti-Chinese Movement

COOLIDGE, MARY ROBERTS, *Chinese Immigration* (New York, 1909).

CRANE, PAUL, and LARSON, ALFRED, "The Chinese Massacre," *Annals of Wyoming*, Vol. XII (1940), pp. 47–55.

DE FELLA, PAUL M., "Lantern in the Western Sky," *Historical Society of Southern California Quarterly*, Vol. XLII (1960), pp. 57–88, 161–185.

DORLAND, CHESTER P., "Chinese Massacre at Los Angeles in 1871," *Historical Society of Southern California Annual*, Vol. III (1894), pp. 22–26.

LOCKLEAR, WILLIAM R., "The Celestials and the Angels," *Historical Society of Southern California Quarterly*, Vol. XLII (1960), pp. 239–256.

"Oriental Immigration," *Outlook*, Vol. LXXVII (1907), pp. 99–100.

SANDMYER, ELMER C., *The Anti-Chinese Movement in California* (Urbana, Illinois, 1939).

STEVENSON, ROBERT LOUIS, *Across the Plains* (New York, 1879). *The Chinese Massacre at Rock Springs, Wyoming Territory* (Boston, 1886).

U.S. House Reports, 49th Cong., 1st sess., Vol. 7, No. 2044 (Washington, D.C., 1885–1886).

Frontier and Vigilante Justice

BANCROFT, HUBERT H., *Popular Tribunals*, 2 vols. (San Francisco, 1887; New York, 1967).

BIRNEY, HOFFMAN, *Vigilantes* (Philadelphia, 1929).

BLACK, PAUL W., "Lynchings in Iowa," *Iowa Journal of History and Politics*, Vol. X (1912), pp. 151–209.

BROWN, RICHARD M., "The American Vigilante Tradition," *Violence in America: Historical and Comparative Perspectives*, A Report Submitted to the National Commission on the Causes and Prevention of Violence (New York, 1969), Chapter 5.

——— "Pivot of American Vigilantism: The San Francisco Vigilance Committee of 1856," in John A. Carroll, ed., *Reflections of Western Historians* (Tuscon, 1969).

CAUGHEY, JOHN W., *Their Majesties the Mob* (Chicago, 1960).

CLARK, WALTER VAN TILBURG, *The Ox Bow Incident* (New York, 1940).

COATES, ROBERT M., *The Outlaw Years* (New York, 1930).

CUTLER, JAMES E., *Lynch Law* (New York, 1905).

DAVIDSON, LEVETTE J., "A Ballad of the Wyoming Rustler War," *Western Folklore*, Vol. VI (1947), pp. 115–118.

DAVIS, HARTLEY, and SMYTH, CLIFFORD, "The Land of the Feuds," *Munsey's Magazine*, Vol. XXX (1903), pp. 161–172.

FRANTZ, JOE B., "The Frontier Tradition: An Invitation to Violence," *Violence in America: Historical and Comparative Perspectives*, A Report Submitted to the National Commission on the Causes and Prevention of Violence (New York, 1969), Chapter 4.

GARD, WAYNE, *Frontier Justice* (Norman, Oklahoma, 1949).

GLENN, SHIRLEY, *Law West of Fort Smith* (New York, 1957).

GUERNSY, CHARLES A., *Wyoming Cowboy Days* (New York, 1936).

HOLDEN, WILLIAM C., "Law and Lawlessness on the Texas Frontier," *Southwestern Historical Quarterly*, Vol. XLIV (1940), pp. 188–203.

HOLT, R. D., "The Introduction of Barbed Wire Into Texas and the Fence-Cutting War," *West Texas Historical Association Year Book*, Vol. VI (1930), pp. 65–79.

HOUGH, EMERSON, *The Story of the Cowboy* (New York, 1897).

LANGFORD, NATHANIEL PITT, *Vigilante Days and Ways*, 2 vols. (Boston, 1890).

MERCER, A. S., *The Banditti of the Plains* (San Francisco, 1953).

OLMSTED, FREDERICK LAW, *Journey Through Texas* (New York, 1857).

RISTER, CARL C., *Southern Plainsmen* (Norman, Oklahoma, 1938).

SMITH, HELENA H., *The War on Powder River* (New York, 1966).

SONNICHSEN, CHARLES L., *I'll Die Before I Run* (New York, 1962).

STECHNESSER, KENT L., *The Western History in Western Legend* (Norman, Oklahoma, 1965).

STUART, GRANVILLE, *Forty Years on the Frontier*, Vol. II (Cleveland, 1925).

TOWNE, CHARLES W., and WENTWORTH, EDWARD N., *Shepards' Empire* (Norman, Oklahoma, 1945).

WILLIAMS, MARY F., *History of the San Francisco Committee of Vigilance of 1851: A Study of Social Control on the California Frontier in the Days of the Gold Rush* (Berkeley, California, 1921).

Labor Struggles

ADAMIC, LOUIS, *Dynamite: The Story of Class Violence in America* (New York, 1931).

ANGLE, PAUL M., *Bloody Williamson* (New York, 1952).

BRISSENDEN, PAUL F., *The I.W.W.: A Study of American Syndicalism* (New York, 1919).

BRUCE, ROBERT V., *1877: Year of Violence* (Indianapolis, 1959).

COMMONS, JOHN R., and associates, *History of Labor in the United States*, 4 vols. (New York, 1918–1935).

CORNELL, ROBERT J., *The Anthracite Coal Strike* (Washington, D.C., 1957).

DAVID, HENRY, *History of the Haymarket Affair* (New York, 1950).

DELAND, L. F., "The Lawrence Strike: A Study," *The Atlantic Monthly*, Vol. CIX (1912), pp. 694–705.

DULLES, FOSTER R., *Labor in America,* 2d. rev. ed. (New York, 1960).

FONER, PHILIP S., *History of the Labor Movement in the United States* (New York, 1947).

FRENCH, GEORGE E., "The Coeur d'Alene Riots," *Overland Monthly,* Vol. XXVI (1895), pp. 32–49.

GUTMAN, HERBERT G., "The Tompkins Square Riot in New York City," *Labor History,* Vol. II (Winter, 1955), pp. 44–70.

"Industrial Warfare," *Fortune,* Vol. XVI (November, 1937), pp. 104–111.

JENSON, VERNON H., *Heritage of Conflict* (Ithaca, New York, 1950).

LAMPMAN, BEN HUR, *Centralia Tragedy and Trial* (Tacoma, Washington, 1920).

LEUCHTENBURG, WILLIAM E., *The Perils of Prosperity: 1914–1932* (Chicago, 1958).

LINDSEY, ALMONT, *The Pullman Strike: The Story of a Unique Experiment and of a Great Labor Upheaval* (Chicago, 1942).

McCABE, JAMES D., (Edward W. Martin), *The History of the Great Riots* (Philadelphia, 1877).

PINKOWSKI, EDWARD, *The Latimer Massacre* (Philadelphia, 1950).

SMITH, WALKER C., *The Everett Massacre* (Chicago, 1917).

U.S. House Report, "Investigation of Labor Troubles in Missouri, Kansas, Texas and Illinois," 49th Cong., 2d sess., Doc. No. 4174 (Washington, D.C., 1887).

U.S. House Report, "Labor Troubles in the Anthracite Region of Pennsylvania," 50th Cong., 2d sess., Doc. No. 4147 (Washington, D.C., 1889).

U.S. Senate, "Report on the Chicago Strike of June–July 1894, by U.S. Strike Commission," 53d Cong., 3d sess., Ex. Doc. No. 7 (Washington, D.C., 1894).

U.S. Senate, "Report on Labor Disturbances in the State of Colorado from 1880–1904," 58th Cong., 3d sess., Doc. No. 122 (Washington, D.C., 1905).

U.S. House Report, "The Strike at Lawrence, Mass.," 62d Cong., 2d sess., Doc. No. 671 (Washington, D.C., 1912).

U.S. Senate, "Report on Strike of Textile Workers in Lawrence, Mass., in 1912," 62d Cong., 2d sess., Doc. No. 870 (Washington, D.C., 1912).

WARNE, FRANK JULIAN, *The Coal Mine Workers* (New York, 1905).

WHIPPLE, LEON, *The Story of Civil Liberty in the United States* (New York, 1939).

YELLEN, SAMUEL, *American Labor Struggles* (New York, 1936).

ABOUT THE AUTHOR

IRVING SLOAN graduated from the University of Wisconsin and Harvard Law School. After practicing law for a short while, he decided to become a teacher and attended Yeshiva University Graduate School of Education. Since 1961 he has been teaching in the Scarsdale school system. He has been a consultant for Educational Services Institute in Cambridge and the Center for American Liberties at Columbia University. His first book was a reference work entitled *The Negro in Modern American History Textbooks*, published by the American Federation of Teachers. His next book, also published by the AFT, is *The Negro in American Encyclopedias*, to be published in 1970.